SYDNEY

TOP SIGHTS · LOCAL EXPERIENCES

ANDY SYMINGTON

Contents

Plan Your Trip

General Post Office (GPO; p61)
LEONID ANDRONOV/SHUTTERSTOCK ©

Explore Sydney 29

Worth a Trip

Survival Guide 175

Special Features

Welcome to Sydney

Sydney, spectacularly draped around its glorious harbour and beaches, has visual wow factor like few other cities. Scratch the surface and it only gets better. Sydney is exuberant, sassy and stacks of fun, whether you're learning to surf, tramping through marvellous national parks or channeling the city's hedonistic streak in its superb array of eateries.

Sunset over Sydney Harbour Bridge (p36) and the city skyline

ANDY BALASKO/SHUTTERSTOCK ©

Top Sights

Sydney Opera House

Visionary harbourside architectural masterpiece. **p32**

Sydney Harbour Bridge

Harbour crossing and Sydney icon. **p36**

Royal Botanic Garden

Verdant city-centre haven. **p34**

Art Gallery of NSW

Treasure trove of Australian art. **p56**

Chinatown
Fascinating blend of cultures. **p58**

Australian Museum
Grande dame of Sydney museums. **p112**

Bondi Beach

Surf a legendary beach. **p144**

North Head

Fabulous walking; supreme harbour vistas. **p162**

Eating

Sydney's cuisine rivals that of any great world city. The city truly celebrates Australia's place on the Pacific Rim, marrying fresh local ingredients – excellent seafood is a highlight – with the flavours of Asia, the Mediterranean, the Americas and, of course, its colonial past. Sydneysiders are real foodies, always seeking out the latest hot restaurant.

Where to Eat

Sydney's top restaurants are properly pricey, but eating out needn't be expensive. There are plenty of budget ethnic eateries where you can grab a cheap, zingy pizza or a bowl of noodles. Cafes are a good bet for a solid, often adventurous and usually reasonably priced meal. Pubs either do reliable standard fare, often with excellent prices, or casual but high-quality Modern Australian dining. The numerous BYO (bring your own wine) restaurants offer a substantially cheaper eating experience; the Inner West is brimful of them.

Vegetarians & Vegans

Sydney is great for herbivores. Unless you wander into a steakhouse by mistake, vegetarians should have no trouble finding satisfying choices on most menus. Some leading restaurants offer separate vegetarian menus, often stretching to multiple-course degustation.

The more socially progressive suburbs such as Newtown and Glebe have the widest range of veggie options. Surry Hills, Darlinghurst and Kings Cross also have good choices.

Best Restaurants

Quay Inventive fine dining with the best views in Sydney. (p42)

LuMi Inventive Italo-Japanese degustation in a quiet wharfside location in Pyrmont. (p82)

Mr Wong Hip Cantonese joint with perpetual queues out the door. (p68)

Ester Informal but innovative Modern-Australian dining. (p99)

Porteño Delicious slow-cooked meat and bucketloads of atmosphere. (p119)

TIMOTHY CHRISTIANTO/SHUTTERSTOCK ©

Folonomo High-quality not-for-profit eatery. (p120)

Tetsuya's A degustatory journey through multiple inventive courses. (p70)

Best Snacks & Sweets

Cow & the Moon Sydney's best ice-cream. (p93)

Bourke Street Bakery Irresistible pastries, cakes and bread. (p117)

Koi Dessert Bar Unbelievable dessert creations. (p96)

Best Cafes

Single O Still pioneering coffee. (p121)

Grounds of Alexandria Amazing organic farm-cafe. (p95)

Reuben Hills Brunches with a Latin American twist. (p118)

Trio Fight for a seat at this Bondi star. (p153)

Pablo & Rusty's The city centre's best coffee. (p67)

Wedge Narrow but quality-packed Glebe cafe. (p94)

Best Vegetarian & Vegan

Yellow Upmarket vegetarian degustation menus are memorably good. (p138)

Golden Lotus Crisp and fresh Vietnamese vegan fare in Newtown. (p94)

Lentil As Anything Heartening, pay-what-you-want social project. (p94)

Earth to Table Raw, vegan and sugarless creations

work a treat at this cafe. (p152)

Funky Pies Who took the meat out of an Aussie icon? (p152)

Best Seafood

Boathouse on Blackwattle Bay Lovely Glebe location overlooking the water. (p99)

Flying Fish At the end of a Pyrmont pier, and boasting super views. (p84)

Golden Century Meet your meal in the tanks on the way in. (p71)

Azuma Sushi and sashimi of stratospheric quality. (p69)

Drinking & Nightlife

In a city where rum was once the main currency, it's little wonder that drinking plays a big part in the Sydney social scene – whether it's knocking back some tinnies at the beach, schmoozing after work or warming up for a night on the town. Sydney offers plenty of choice in drinking establishments, from the flashy to the trashy.

The Sydney Scene

The relaxation of licensing laws has seen a blooming of 'small bars' in the city centre and inner suburbs. These are great spots, often difficult to find and with a quirky atmosphere, though the drinks don't come cheap.

The local pub, traditionally called a hotel because the liquor laws once meant they had to offer accommodation to serve booze, survives throughout the city. Often on corners, these venerable gems have been improved in recent years by beer gardens, upgraded food menus and a stupendous array of local craft beers.

Door Policies

Sydney's bouncers are often strict, arbitrary and immune to logic. Being questioned and searched every time you want a drink after 8pm on a weekend can definitely take the edge off a Sydney night out.

It is against the law to serve people who are intoxicated and you won't be admitted to a venue if you appear drunk. Expect to be questioned about how much you've had to drink that night.

Be prepared to present photo ID with proof of your age.

Lockouts

In an effort to cut down on alcohol-fuelled violence, tough licensing laws have been introduced to a large area of the central city. Within this zone, licensed venues are not permitted to admit people after 1.30am. However, if you arrive before then, the venue is permitted to continue serving

COOLR/SHUTTERSTOCK ©

you alcohol until 3am, or 3.30am in the case of certain venues which you can enter until 2am.

Best Historic Pubs

Hero of Waterloo Sturdy stone stalwart in the Rocks (p45)

Lord Nelson One of three claiming the title of 'oldest pub'. (p46)

Fortune of War Beautiful front bar. (p47)

Courthouse Hotel A slice of an older Newtown. (p102)

Shakespeare Hotel Gloriously traditional Sydney boozer in Surry Hills. (p124)

Best Outdoor Drinking

Watsons Bay Beach Club Take a ferry to this summer and weekend classic. (p159)

Opera Bar Is there a better-located bar in the world? (Pictured; p45)

Glenmore Roof deck with great Opera House views. (p46)

Beresford Hotel Mixed crowd and quality wine and food. (p124)

Best Small Bars

Baxter Inn Whisky-laden city speakeasy. (p71)

Grandma's Kitsch retro basement hideaway. (p73)

Uncle Ming's Low-lit den of dumplings and cocktails. (p71)

Barber Shop Get a short back and sides on your way in. (p72)

Best Dancefloors

Frankie's Pizza Pizza slices, live bands, a nightclub...who needs more? (p71)

Ivy Glam inner-city location with Sydney's top club night. (p71)

Lazybones Lounge Gloriously louche and welcoming Inner West nightspot. (p100)

Arq Flashy and upmarket club in LGBTQ+ heartland. (p126)

Shopping

Shopping is the number one recreational activity in consumerist Sydney. Retail covers a wide range here, from glitzy city-centre boutiques, to koala-heavy tourist tat, to just-so Paddington galleries and grungy Newtown vintage stores. Best of all are the markets, with a bit of everything and a buzzy weekend scene; an essential Sydney experience.

Shopping Areas

Sydney's city centre is brimming over with department, chain and international fashion stores and arcades – shopping here is about as fast and furious as Australia gets. Paddington is the place for art and fashion, while new and second-hand boutiques around Newtown and Surry Hills cater to a hipper, more alternative crowd. Double Bay, Mosman and Balmain are a bit more 'mother of the bride', and if you're chasing bargains,

head to Chinatown or the Alexandria factory outlets.

Newtown and Glebe have the lion's share of book and record stores. For surf gear, head to Bondi or Manly. Woollahra, Newtown (around St Peters station) and Surry Hills are good for antiques. For souvenirs – from exquisite opals to tacky T-shirts – try the Rocks, Circular Quay and Darling Harbour.

What to Buy

Want something quintessentially Australian

to take home? Head to the Rocks and dig up some opals, an Akubra hat, a Driza-Bone coat or some Blundstone boots. Aboriginal art makes an excellent purchase, but make sure it is ethically sourced.

Sydney has a thriving fashion scene, and a summer dress or Speedos won't eat up luggage space. Ask at music stores or bookshops about local bands and authors. Hunter Valley wine makes a great gift – check your country's duty-free allowance before buying.

KOKKAI NG/GETTY IMAGES ©

Taxes & Refunds

Sales taxes are included in the advertised price. Apart from the 10% goods and services tax (GST), the only other sales duties are on things such as alcohol and tobacco, which are best bought at duty-free shops, such as those at the airport. The GST tourist refund scheme (p182) has mostly replaced traditional duty-free shopping.

Best Markets

Paddington Markets Sydney's most famous market (pictured), selling everything from clothing to palm-reading. (p109)

Bondi Markets Fruit and veg on Saturdays, assorted bric-a-brac on Sundays. (p157)

Glebe Markets One big counter-cultural get-together. (p107)

Carriageworks Farmers Market Foodies flock here on Saturday mornings. (p105)

Best Jewellery

Paspaley Pearls from northwest Australia. (p75)

Opal Minded Get the classic Aussie gemstone. (p49)

Best Aboriginal Art

Gannon House Gallery Inspiring selection in the Rocks. (p49)

Artery Great range, from original works to printed souvenirs. (p127)

Karlangu Wide selection near Wynyard station. (p75)

Best Bookshops

Gleebooks Well-loved Glebe bookshop, with regular author talks. (p106)

Abbey's Brilliant inner-city bookshop, especially good on history, languages and sci-fi. (p74)

Better Read Than Dead Well-presented and -stocked Newtown store. (p107)

Entertainment

Take Sydney at face value and you might unfairly stereotype its good citizens as shallow and a little narcissistic. But take a closer look: the arts scene is thriving, sophisticated and progressive – it's not an accident that Sydney's icon is an opera house!Spectator sports, led by rugby league, are huge and attending a match is highly recommended.

Classical Music & Opera

There's a passionate audience for classical music in Sydney. Without having the extensive repertoires of European cities, Sydney offers plenty of inspired classical performances – the perfect excuse to check out the interior of the famous harbourside sails of the Sydney Opera House (p32). The City Recital Hall (p73) is another venue, with excellent acoustics.

Australia has produced some of the world's most ear-catching opera singers, including Dames Nellie Melba and Joan Sutherland.

Live Bands

Since the 1950s Sydney has been hip to jazz, and in the 1970s and '80s, Aussie pub rock became a force to be reckoned with. Sydney's live-music scene took a hell of a hit in the 1990s, when lucrative poker machines were first allowed in pubs, and hasn't really recovered. That said, you can catch bands any night of the week in various pubs, especially around the Inner West. Check the free street mags (*The Music* is the best; www.themusic.com.au) and Friday's *Sydney Morning Herald* for listings.

Spectator Sports

Australia's national self-esteem is so thoroughly intertwined with sporting success that locals worship their teams as they would a religion. Sport dominates weekend TV schedules, but nothing beats catching a game live.

PHOTOGRAPH BY DAVID MESSENT/GETTY IMAGES ©

Rugby league is Sydney's all-consuming passion: a superfast, super-macho game with a frenzied atmosphere for spectators.

In rugby union and cricket, whipping the Kiwis, Poms and South Africans into submission is the name of the game, while in the national Australian Football League (AFL) and soccer competitions, Sydney's teams hold their own.

Women's sport has traditionally been underfunded and underwatched, but has an increasingly high profile as sports-mad Sydney gradually wakes up to it.

Best Entertainment Venues

Sydney Opera House Don't miss a chance to see the House in action. (p48)

State Theatre We don't care what's on – visiting this beautiful place (pictured) is a joy. (p74)

City Recital Hall The city's premier classical-music venue. (p73)

Belvoir St Theatre Consistently excellent productions in an intimate setting. (p127)

Best Places for Live Bands

Oxford Art Factory Live indie bands, DJs and assorted bohemian happenings. (p127)

Lansdowne Hotel Bands upstairs most nights. (p104)

Bald Faced Stag Friendly Leichhardt pub for rock and metal. (p104)

Camelot Lounge Two separate stages with interesting programming. (p104)

Metro Theatre Excellent sightlines and acoustics for midsize touring rock acts. (p73)

Beaches

The beach is an essential part of the Sydney experience. Sydney's ocean beaches broadly divide into the eastern beaches, running south of the harbour from Bondi onwards, and the northern beaches, north of the harbour, starting at Manly. The numerous harbour beaches are mostly east of the bridge on both the north and south sides.

AI_YOSHI/GETTY IMAGES ©

Need to Know

Always swim between the red-and-yellow flags on lifesaver-patrolled beaches.

If you get into trouble, hold up your hand to signal to the lifesavers.

Due to pollution from stormwater drains, avoid swimming in the ocean for a day and in the harbour for three days after heavy rains.

Ocean Pools

Sydney is blessed with a string of 40 man-made ocean pools up and down the coast, most of them free. Some, like Mahon Pool (pictured; p151), are what are known as bogey holes – natural-looking rock pools where you can safely splash about and snorkel, even while the surf surges in. Others are more like swimming pools; Bondi's Icebergs (p145) is a good example of this kind. They normally close one day a week so they can clean the seaweed out.

Best Beaches

Bondi Beach Australia's most iconic ocean beach. (p144)

Nielsen Park The pick of the harbour beaches, surrounded by beautiful national park. (p159)

Bronte Beach Family-friendly and backed by a park, this is an Eastern Suburbs gem. (p150)

Whale Beach Peachy-coloured sand and crashing waves; you've really left the city behind at this stunning Northern Beaches haven. (p173)

For Kids

SAKARET/SHUTTERSTOCK ©

Active Pursuits

Many surf schools offer lessons for kids; bike tours are another good way to expend excess energy, as are the rope courses at Sydney Olympic Park and Taronga Zoo.

Sydney Harbour Kayaks (www.sydney harbourkayaks.com. au; Smiths Boat Shed, 81 Parriwi Rd, Mosman) welcomes accompanied 12-year-olds to its tours and also rents kayaks to families with kids as young as three.

Indoor Options

Kids adore Ultimo's science- and technology-focused Powerhouse Museum. Close by at Darling Harbour, tweens are likely to be quite distracted by Rihanna at Madame Tussauds. Across town, the Australian Museum is a real hit with the younger crowd, especially its excellent dinosaur exhibition. You'll be surprised by the child-friendly Art Gallery of NSW; there are also regular art safaris and creative workshops at the Museum of Contemporary Art. The delights of the Sydney Opera House aren't restricted to adults. Little astronomers might want to do some stargazing at the very kid-focused Sydney Observatory.

Babysitting

Most big hotels offer services. Otherwise agencies can send babysitters to you, usually for a four-hour minimum (per hour from $25) and a booking fee (from $23).

Best For Kids

Royal Botanic Garden (pictured) Room to romp in this scenic park. (p34)

Sydney Sea Life Aquarium An underwater world to discover. (p81)

Australian National Maritime Museum Clamber around a submarine. (p79)

Powerhouse Museum A broad collection for all ages. (p92)

Taronga Zoo Meet Australia's native fauna. (p51)

Australian Museum Dinosaurs are just the beginning. (p112)

Luna Park A time-honoured funfair. (p51)

Sydney Observatory Bring out the budding astronomer. (p40)

LGBTQ+ Sydney

CATHERINE SUTHERLAND/LONELY PLANET ©

Sydney's LGBTQ+ community is visible, vibrant and an integral part of the city's social fabric. Partly because central Sydney is so well integrated, and partly because of smartphone apps facilitating contact, the gay nightlife scene has died off substantially. But the action's still going on and Sydney is indisputably one of the world's great queer cities.

Mardi Gras

The **Sydney Gay & Lesbian Mardi Gras** (www.mardigras.org.au) is now the biggest tourist-attracting date on the Australian calendar. While the straights focus on the parade, the gay and lesbian community throws itself into the entire festival, including the blitzkrieg of partying that surrounds it. The parade and party are held on the first Saturday in March.

Acceptance

The battle for social acceptance of the LGBTQ+ community has been long and protracted, but successful. The 2017 postal survey on gay marriage, which resulted in its legalisation, nevertheless revealed a significant split between conservative and liberal areas of Sydney on the issue.

Best LGBTQ+ Venues

Arq The city's hottest gay dancefloor. (p126)

Imperial Hotel The legendary home of Priscilla, Queen of the Desert. (p103)

Palms on Oxford Good-time, trashy, camp dance venue. (p126)

Best LGBTQ+ Shopping

Bookshop Darlinghurst Longstanding gay bookshop and a great source of local information. (p129)

Sax Fetish Racks of shiny black leather and rubber gear. (p128)

Gertrude & Alice Named after literary lesbians and packed with interesting reads. (p157)

Best Lesbian Hangouts

Sly Fox Hosts Sydney's longest-running lesbian night, every Wednesday. (p103)

McIver's Baths Coogee's legendary women-only sea baths. (p151)

Historic Buildings

LKPRO/SHUTTERSTOCK ©

Best Colonial Gems

Vaucluse House William Wentworth's Vaucluse mansion is a rare surviving colonial estate on the harbour's edge. (p159)

Elizabeth Bay House Another harbourside home, built in a gracious Georgian style in the heart of Lizzie Bay. (p135)

Hyde Park Barracks Museum Convict architect Francis Greenway's beautiful convict accommodation, housing a fascinating museum. (p64)

Old Government House Part of an important cluster of remnants of the early colony in Parramatta. (p53)

Queen Victoria Building The most unrestrained and ornate survivor of the Victorian era. (Pictured; p64)

Martin Place A stretch of grand bank buildings and the High Victorian–style former General Post Office,

the most iconic building of its time. (p61)

Elizabeth Farm Sydney's oldest colonial house is part of this early farmhouse. (p53)

Susannah Place Museum These tenement buildings at the Rocks give great insight into historic life there. (p40)

Best Religious Buildings

St Mary's Cathedral Beamed in from Gothic Europe, the grand Catholic cathedral is awash with colour when the sun hits its stained glass. (p65)

Great Synagogue A mismatch of architectural styles, maybe, but a beautiful one. (p67)

St James' Church Francis Greenway's elegant, understated church is perhaps his crowning achievement. (p66)

Best Industrial Remnants

Powerhouse Museum This building once generated power for the tram network and is now a shrine to technology and innovation. (p92)

Cockatoo Island The detritus of defunct shipyards lends a sculptural quality to the island landscape. (p53)

Walsh Bay Elegant Edwardian warehouses, once part of a bustling port, now housing theatres, restaurants and apartments. (p41)

Woolloomooloo Wharf The wool bales may have gone, but the winches and girders remain. (p135)

Carriageworks Huge brick train sheds converted into an edgy arts precinct. (p92)

Tramsheds The former depot for Sydney's old trams; now a foodie precinct accessible via the new light rail network. (p98)

Four Perfect Days

Day One

Start at Circular Quay and head directly to **Sydney Opera House** (p32). Circle around it and follow the shoreline into the **Royal Botanic Garden** (p34). Have a good look around and then continue around **Mrs Macquaries Point** (p35) and along to the **Art Gallery of NSW** (p56), taking a detour into Woolloomooloo if you fancy some lunch. Take some time to explore the gallery then cross the **Domain** and cut through **Sydney Hospital** to Macquarie St. **Parliament House** (p61) is immediately to the right, while to the left is **The Mint** and **Hyde Park Barracks** (pictured; p64). Cross into **Hyde Park** (p61) and head straight through its centre, crossing Park St and continuing on to the **Anzac Memorial** (p66).

Day Two

THORSTEN RUST/SHUTTERSTOCK ©

Grab your swimming gear and head to the beach. Catch the bus to **Bondi Beach** (pictured; p144) and spend some time strolling about and soaking it all in. If the weather's right, stop for a swim in the sea or at **Icebergs Pool** (p145). Once you're done, take the **clifftop path** (p150) to **Tamarama** (p150) and on to **Bronte** (p150), both lovely bits of sand. Continue on the coastal path through **Waverley Cemetery** (p150) and down to **Clovelly** (p150). This is a great spot to stop for a swim or a snorkel. Continuing on you'll pass **Gordons Bay** and **Dolphin Point** before you arrive at **Coogee Beach** (p150), where you'll find lots of places to swim and some good spots for a beer afterwards.

Day Three

MAGSPACE/SHUTTERSTOCK ©

Take a ferry from Circular Quay to **Watsons Bay** (p158). Watch the waves pound the cliffs at **The Gap** (p159), then continue on to **Camp Cove** (p159) for a dip. Take the **South Head Heritage Trail** (p159) for sublime views of the city and the harbour. After lunch, head back to Circular Quay and explore the Rocks. Start at the **Museum of Contemporary Art** (p40) and then head up into the network of lanes to the **Rocks Discovery Museum** (p40). Go through the Argyle Cut to **Millers Point** and up **Observatory Hill**. Pop into one of Sydney's oldest pubs – try the **Lord Nelson** (p46) or the **Hero of Waterloo** (pictured; p45) – then explore the wharves of **Walsh Bay** (p41), and double back under **Sydney Harbour Bridge** (p36).

Day Four

Have a stroll around the Darling Harbour waterfront and settle on whichever of the big attractions takes your fancy – perhaps the **Australian National Maritime Museum** (p79). Each of these will easily fill an entire morning. Next, jump on the river service at King St Wharf and take an hour-long cruise upstream as far as **Sydney Olympic Park**. Take a stroll around **Newington Nature Reserve** until the next ferry arrives to whisk you back. Stop at **Cockatoo Island** (pictured; p53) for a look at its art installations and the remnants of its convict and shipbuilding past. From here you can head back to Darling Harbour or Circular Quay.

Need to Know

For detailed information, see Survival Guide (p174)

Currency
Australian dollar ($)

Language Spoken
English

Visas
All visitors to Australia need a visa. New Zealand nationals receive a visa on arrival.

Money
ATMs are everywhere and major credit cards are widely accepted.

Mobile Phones
Local SIM cards are cheap. Using mobiles while driving is prohibited unless hands-free.

Time
Eastern Standard Time (GMT/UTC plus 10 hours)

Plugs & Adaptors
Standard voltage is 220 to 240 volts AC (50Hz). Plugs are flat three-pin types.

Tipping
If restaurant service is good, it is customary to tip (up to 10%).

Daily Budget

Budget: Less than $190
Dorm beds: $30–50
Return train trip: $8
Hanging out at the beach: free
Pizza, pasta, noodles or burgers: $10–20

Midrange: $190–320
Private room with own bathroom: $150–250
Cafe breakfast: $20–25
All-day public transport: maximum $15.40 using Opal card
Two-course dinner with glass of wine: $50–70

Top End: More than $320
Four-star hotel: from $250
Three-course dinner in top restaurant with wine: $140–250
Opera ticket: $160–350
Taxis: $50

Useful Websites

Destination NSW (www.sydney.com) Official visitors guide.

TripView The handiest app for planning public transport journeys.

Time Out (www.timeout.com/sydney) 'What's on' information and reviews.

Not Quite Nigella (www.notquite nigella.com) Entertaining food blog.

FBI Radio (https://fbiradio.com) Underground music and arts scene coverage.

Lonely Planet (www.lonelyplanet.com/sydney) Destination information, hotel bookings, traveller forum and more.

Arriving in Sydney

Most people arrive in Sydney by air, though you can arrive by bus and train from other Australian cities.

✈ Sydney Airport

10km south of city centre.

Taxis to the city cost up to $55 and depart from the front of the terminals

Airport shuttles head to city hotels for around $20

Trains depart from beneath the terminal but charge a whopping $13.80 on top of the normal train fare for the short journey into the city

🚃 Central Station

Country and interstate **trains** arrive at Central station, at the southern end of the city centre. Follow the signs downstairs to connect to local services or head to Railway Sq for buses.

🚃 Sydney Coach Terminal

Long-distance **coaches** stop in front of Central station.

⚓ Overseas Passenger Terminal

Many **cruise ships** pull in here, right on Circular Quay. There's a train station nearby.

Getting Around

Transport NSW (☎131 500; www.transportnsw.info) coordinates all of the state-run bus, ferry, train and light-rail services. The system-wide Opal transport card is necessary for travel. The TripView app is very useful for real-time public transport info and journey planning.

🚃 Train

The linchpin of the network, with lines radiating out from Central station.

🚃 Buses

Particularly useful for getting to the beaches and parts of the Inner West

⚓ Ferries

Head all around the harbour and up the river to Parramatta.

🚃 Light Rail (Tram)

Handy for Pyrmont and Glebe; from 2019, city-hopping, Surry Hills, Moore Park and Randwick.

M Metro

Under construction. The first line will link northwestern Sydney with Chatswood from 2019; the second phase will through the city centre and out to the west by the mid 2020s.

Advance Planning

Three months before Book accommodation; make sure your passport, visa and travel insurance are in order.

One month before Book top restaurants; check to see if your visit coincides with any major cultural or sporting events and book tickets.

A week before Top up your credit cards; check the Sydney news sites and 'what's on' lists.

Sydney Neighbourhoods

City Centre & Haymarket (p55)
Sydney's central business district offers plenty of choices for shopping, eating and sightseeing, with colonial buildings scattered among the skyscrapers.

Darling Harbour & Pyrmont (p77)
Unashamedly tourist focused, Darling Harbour tempts visitors to its shoreline bars and restaurants with fireworks displays and a sprinkling of glitz.

Inner West (p87)
Quietly bohemian Glebe and more loudly bohemian Newtown are the best known of the Inner West's tightly packed suburbs, which begin at the University of Sydney.

Sydney Harbour Bridge

Sydney Opera House

Royal Botanic Garden

Art Gallery of NSW

Chinatown

Australian Museum

Surry Hills & Darlinghurst (p111)
Home to a mishmash of inner-city hipsters, yuppies, a large LGBTQ+ community, and an array of excellent bars and eateries.

North Head

Circular Quay & the Rocks (p31)
The historic heart of Sydney, containing its most famous sights.

Manly (p161)
The only place in Sydney where you can catch a ferry to swim in the ocean, Manly caps off the harbour with scrappy charm.

Kings Cross & Potts Point (p131)
Strip joints, tacky tourist shops and backpacker hostels bang heads with classy restaurants, boozy bars and gorgeous guesthouses.

Bondi to Coogee (p143)
Improbably goodlooking arcs of sand framed by jagged cliffs, the eastern beaches are a big part of the Sydney experience.

Bondi Beach

Explore
Sydney

Worth a Trip 🔭

Sydney's Walking Tours 🥾

Sky Safari cable car (p51) CONSTANTIN STANCIU/SHUTTERSTOCK ©

Explore ⬡

Circular Quay & the Rocks

The birthplace of both the city and the current nation, this compact area seamlessly combines the historic with the exuberantly modern. Join the tourist pilgrimage to the Opera House and Harbour Bridge, then grab a schooner at a convict-era pub in the Rocks.

Sydney Cove carries the twin stars of the city's iconography, with the Harbour Bridge (p36) and the Opera House (p32) abutting each end of its horseshoe. Circular Quay's promenade serves as a backdrop for buskers of mixed merit and locals disgorging from harbour ferries. The Rocks is unrecognisable from the squalid place it once was and now serves as an 'olde-worlde' tourist focus. Over the ridge is Millers Point, a low-key colonial district that makes a calming diversion from the harbourside tourist fray, and Walsh Bay, a handsome redeveloped maritime precinct.

Getting There & Around

🚆 Circular Quay is one of the City Circle train stations; Wynyard is also close by.

⛴ Circular Quay is Sydney's ferry hub, providing services all around the harbour.

🚌 Circular Quay is a terminus for several eastern suburbs bus routes.

🚋 From 2019, light rail will travel from Circular Quay along George St to Central station and beyond.

Circular Quay & the Rocks Map on p38

The Rocks district (p43) at dusk M. LETSCHERT/SHUTTERSTOCK ©

Top Sight 📷
Sydney Opera House

Gazing upon the Sydney Opera House with virgin eyes is a sure way to send a tingle down your spine. Gloriously curvaceous and pointy, this landmark perches dramatically at the tip of Bennelong Point, waiting for its close-up. No matter from which angle you point a lens at it, it shamelessly mugs for the camera; it really doesn't have a bad side.

◉ **MAP P38, G3**

📞 02-9250 7111

www.sydneyopera house.com

Bennelong Point

tours adult/child $37/20

🕐 tours 9am-5pm

🚉 Circular Quay

Design & Construction

Danish architect Jørn Utzon's competition-winning 1956 design is Australia's most recognisable visual image. It's said to have been inspired by billowing sails, orange segments, palm fronds and Mayan temples, and has been likened to nuns in a rugby scrum, a typewriter stuffed with scallop shells and the sexual congress of turtles. It's not until you get close that you realise the seemingly solid expanse of white is actually composed of tiles – 1,056,000 self-cleaning cream-coloured Swedish tiles, to be exact.

Interior

Inside, dance, concerts, opera and theatre are staged in the **Concert Hall**, **Joan Sutherland Theatre**, **Drama Theatre** and **Playhouse**, while more intimate and left-of-centre shows inhabit the **Studio**. The acoustics in the concert hall are superb; the internal aesthetics like the belly of a whale.

Most events (2400 of them annually!) sell out quickly, but partial-view tickets are often available on short notice. The free monthly *What's On* brochure, available at tourist information points and at the Opera House itself, lists upcoming events, including info on the excellent children's programming – a pint-sized entertainment roster of music, drama and dance.

Tours

One-hour guided tours of the interior (adult/child $37/20) depart throughout the day. Not all tours can visit all theatres because of rehearsals, but you're more likely to see everything if you go early. A highlight is the **Utzon Room**, the only part of the Opera House to have an interior designed by the great man himself. For a more in-depth nose around, the two-hour, early-morning backstage tour ($169, departs 7am) includes the Green Room, stars' dressing rooms, stage and orchestra pit.

★ Top Tips

o Renovation works will be taking place through to 2021. Performance schedules and guided tours may be disrupted, so it's worth checking ahead to see how your visit may be affected.

✕ Take a Break

One of Sydney's finest restaurants, Aria (p43), is just opposite the Opera House; perfect for a gourmet pre- or post-show meal.

Opera Bar (p45), on the concourse below the Opera House, is a fabulous spot for a drink or a meal by the water.

Top Sight 📷
Royal Botanic Garden

This expansive park is the inner city's favourite picnic destination, jogging route and snuggling spot. Following the shore of Farm Cove, the bay immediately southeast of the Opera House, the garden was established in 1816 and features plant life from Australia and around the world. It also includes the site of the colony's first paltry vegetable patch.

⊙ **MAP P38, H5**

📞 02-9231 8111

www.rbgsyd.nsw.gov.au

Mrs Macquarie's Rd

admission free

🕒 7am-dusk

🚇 Circular Quay

Collections

Highlights include the rose garden, the rainforest walk, and the succulent garden. The striking Calyx pavilion incorporates a cool, curving glasshouse space with a living wall of greenery that requires some 18,000 plants to fill. It hosts temporary exhibitions on botanical themes.

Government House

Surrounded by English-style grounds, **Government House** (☎ 02-9228 4111; www.governor.nsw. gov.au; Macquarie St; admission free; ⏱ grounds 10am-4pm, tours 10.30am-3pm Fri-Sun) is a Gothic sandstone mansion (built 1837–43), which serves as the official residence of the Governor of NSW. Its lovely loggia looks over a formal garden with the Opera House looming close by.

Mrs Macquaries Point

Mrs Macquaries Point forms the northeastern tip of Farm Cove and provides beautiful views over the bay to the Opera House and city skyline. It was named in 1810 after Elizabeth, Governor Macquarie's wife, who ordered a seat chiselled into the rock from which she could view the harbour. **Mrs Macquaries Chair**, as it's known, remains to this day.

Walks and Tours

Free guided walks depart daily from the information booth outside the Garden Shop. You can also download self-guided tours from the RBG website. The park's paths are mostly wheelchair accessible.

Long before the convicts arrived, this was an initiation ground for the Gadigal (Cadigal) people. Book ahead for the **Aboriginal Heritage Tour** (☎ 02-9231 8134; www.rbgsyd.nsw.gov.au; adult $40; ⏱ 10am Wed, Fri & Sat), which covers local history, traditional plant uses and bush-food tastings.

★ Top Tips

o Estimated walking times on signs are pessimistic. If a sign says something is five minutes away, bank on two.

o If you're all walked out, take a ride on the **Choochoo Express** (www.choochoo.com. au; adult/child $10/5; ⏱ 11am-4pm May-Sep, 10am-4.30pm Oct-Apr), a trackless train that departs from Queen Elizabeth II Gate (nearest the Opera House) every half-hour.

✖ Take a Break

In the park itself, the **Botanic Gardens Restaurant** (☎ 02-9241 2419; www.botanic restaurant.com.au; lunch mains $29-34; ⏱ noon-3pm Mon-Fri, from 9.30am Sat & Sun) offers quality food in a foresty environment.

End your stroll at the wharf at Woolloomooloo, where China Doll (p139) is an excellent venue for waterside dining.

Top Sight

Sydney Harbour Bridge

Whether they're driving over it, climbing up it, jogging across it, shooting fireworks off it or sailing under it, Sydneysiders adore their bridge and swarm around it like ants on ice cream. Dubbed the 'coathanger', the harbour bridge is a spookily big object — moving around town, you'll catch sight of it out of the corner of your eye when you least expect it.

◎ MAP P38, E1

🚉 Circular Quay, Milsons Point

Structure

At 134m high, 1149m long, 49m wide and weighing 52,800 tonnes, Sydney Harbour Bridge is the largest and heaviest (but not the longest) steel arch in the world. It links the Rocks with North Sydney, crossing the harbour at one of its narrowest points. The two halves of chief engineer JJC Bradfield's mighty arch were built outwards from each shore. In 1930, after seven years of toil by 1400 workers, the two arches were only centimetres apart when 100km/h winds set them swaying. The coathanger hung tough, though; the arch was bolted together and the bridge finally opened to the public two years later.

BridgeClimb

Once only painters and daredevils scaled the Harbour Bridge – now anyone with a moderate level of fitness can do it. Make your way through the **BridgeClimb** (☏02-8274 7777; www.bridge climb.com; 3 Cumberland St; adult $258-383, child $178-273) departure lounge and the extensive training session, don your headset, an umbilical safety cord and a dandy grey jumpsuit and up you go. Tours last 2¼ to 3½ hours – a pre-climb toilet stop is a smart idea. The priciest climbs are at dawn and sunset. A cheaper, 90-minute 'sampler' climb (heading to a lower point) is also available, as is an 'express climb', which ascends to the top via a faster route.

Pylon Lookout Museum

The bridge's hefty pylons may look as though they're shouldering all the weight, but they're largely decorative – right down to their granite facing. There are awesome views from **Pylon Lookout** (☏02-9240 1100; www.pylonlookout.com. au; adult/child $15/8.50; ⏱10am-5pm), atop the southeast pylon. Inside the pylon there are exhibits about the bridge's construction, including an eight-minute film that screens every 15 minutes.

★ Top Tips

o The best way to experience the bridge is on foot – don't expect much of a view crossing by train or car (driving south there's a toll).

o Staircases access the bridge from both shores; a footpath runs along its eastern side and a cycleway along the west.

o The northern end of the bridge walk is very close to Milsons Point train station. Walking north to south offers the best views.

✗ Take a Break

The southern end of the bridge sits right among some of the best pubs in the Rocks. Try the rooftop at the Glenmore (p46) for more great views.

If it's a cafe you're after, make your way down to the Fine Food Store (p42), tucked away on a side street.

Circular Quay & the Rocks Sydney Harbour Bridge

N

0 ———— 400 m
0 ———— 0.2 miles

Walsh Bay

Dawes Point

Pier 1

Piers 2 & 3

21

13

Piers 4 & 5

30

Piers 6 & 7

Walsh Bay 5

Piers 8 & 9

10

Hickson Rd

DAWES POINT

Barangaroo Reserve 7

P

Lower Fort St

George

Windmill Steps

Windmill St 17

Trinity Ave

Bradfield Hwy

Cumberland St

36

23

20

Kent St

Argyle La

Argyle Pl

Argyle St

Watson Rd

Bridge Access Stairs

Argyle St 18

22

14

27

25

THE ROCK

MILLERS POINT

1 Sydney Observatory

Susannah Place Museum 3

26

BARANGAROO

Harrington St

Hickson Rd

SH Ervin Gallery 8

Western Distributor

Cumberland St

19

Essex St

George St

Jenkins St

Kent St

Gloucester St

Grosvenor St

Lang Park

Lang St

Dalley St

Grosven St

George St

Barangaroo

Clarence St

York St

Jamison St

E **F** **G** **H**

1

For reviews see
◉ Top Sights		p32
◉ Sights		p40
✕ Eating		p42
🍷 Drinking		p45
☆ Entertainment		p48
🔒 Shopping		p49

Sydney Harbour
Bridge

Dawes
Point
Park

*Sydney Harbour
(Port Jackson)*

2

Campbells
Cove

Bennelong
Point

Sydney Harbour Tunnel

11
✕ Overseas
Passenger
Terminal

☆28
◉
Sydney
Opera
House

🍷16

3

35
🔒33

cks Discovery Museum

✕12

*Sydney
Cove*

useum of
ontemporary Art
4

Circular Quay East

Macquarie St

Government
House

4

rst
eet
ark

Sydney
Ferries

Circular
🍷 Quay

*Royal
Botanic
Garden*
◉

5

ahill 🚇 Expwy
Circular
Quay
i ✕15

Alfred St

Albert St

◉ 6
Justice
& Police
Museum

Pitt St

Reiby Pl

🍷
24

Loftus St

Young St

Phillip St

🔒34

Bridge St

29
☆

Conservatorium Rd

31☆

6

Bent St

Phillip St

Macquarie St

E **F** **G** **H**

Sights

Sydney Observatory

OBSERVATORY

1 ◉ MAP P38, C4

Built in the 1850s, Sydney's copper-domed, Italianate sandstone observatory squats atop **Observatory Hill**, overlooking the harbour. Inside is a collection of vintage apparatus, including Australia's oldest working telescope (1874), as well as background on Australian astronomy and transits of Venus. Also on offer (weekends and school holidays) are child-focused tours (adult/child $10/8), including a solar telescope viewing and planetarium show. Bookings are essential for night-time stargazing sessions, which come in family-oriented (adult/child $22/17) and adult (adult/child $27/20) versions. (☏02-9217 0111; www.maas.museum/sydney-observatory; 1003 Upper Fort St; admission free; ◷10am-5pm; ⛴Circular Quay)

Rocks Discovery Museum

MUSEUM

2 ◉ MAP P38, D4

Divided into four displays – Warrane (pre-1788), Colony (1788–1820), Port (1820–1900) and Transformations (1900 to the present) – this small, excellent museum, tucked away down a Rocks laneway, digs deep into the area's history on an artefact-rich tour. Sensitive attention is given to the Rocks' original inhabitants, the Gadigal (Cadigal) people, and there are interesting tales of early colonial characters. (☏02-9240 8680; www.therocks.com; Kendall Lane; admission free; ◷10am-5pm; ♿; ⛴Circular Quay)

Susannah Place Museum

MUSEUM

3 ◉ MAP P38, D4

Dating from 1844, this diminutive terrace of four houses and a shop selling historical wares is a fascinating time capsule of life in the Rocks. After watching a short film about the past inhabitants, you will be guided through the claustrophobic homes, decorated to reflect different eras. The visit lasts an hour. Groups are limited to eight, so book ahead. (☏bookings 02-9251 5988; www.sydneyliving museums.com.au; 58-64 Gloucester St; adult/child $12/8; ◷tours 2pm, 3pm & 4pm; ⛴Circular Quay)

Museum of Contemporary Art

GALLERY

4 ◉ MAP P38, E4

The MCA is a showcase for Australian and international contemporary art, with a rotating permanent collection and temporary exhibitions. Aboriginal art features prominently. The art-deco building has had a modern space grafted on to it, the highlight of which is the rooftop cafe with stunning views. There are free guided tours daily, with several languages available. (MCA; ☏02-9245 2400; www.

Sydney Observatory

mca.com.au; 140 George St; admission free; ☺9am-5pm Wed, from 10am Thu-Tue; ⊞Circular Quay)

Walsh Bay
WATERFRONT

5 ◉ MAP P38, C2

This section of Dawes Point waterfront was Sydney's busiest before the advent of container shipping and the construction of port facilities at Botany Bay. This century has seen the Federation-era wharves gentrified beyond belief, morphing into luxury hotels, apartments, theatre spaces, power-boat marinas and restaurants. It's a picturesque place to stroll, combining the wharves and harbour views with Barangaroo Park. (www. walshbaysydney.com.au; Hickson Rd; ⊞324, 325, ⊞Wynyard)

Justice & Police Museum
MUSEUM

6 ◉ MAP P38, F5

In a sandstone building that once headquartered the Water Police, this atmospheric museum plunges you straight into Sydney noir. An assemblage of black-and-white photos from police archives provide the backdrop for stories of gangs, murders, bushranging and underworld figures, as well as being a fascinating window into social history. The highlight is the magnificently laconic commentary on the audiovisual features. (☎02-9252 1144; www.sydneyliving museums.com.au; cnr Albert & Phillip Sts; adult/child $12/8; ☺10am-5pm Sat & Sun; ⊞Circular Quay)

Barangaroo Reserve   PARK

7 ◉ MAP P38, A3

Part of Barangaroo, the major redevelopment project of what was a commercial port, this park sits on a headland with wonderful harbour perspectives. The tiered space combines quarried sandstone blocks and native trees and plants to good effect. A lift connecting the park's three levels is good for weary legs. There's a car park under it, and an exhibition space. (www.barangaroo.com; Hickson Rd; 📮324, 325, 🚉Circular Quay)

SH Ervin Gallery   GALLERY

8 ◉ MAP P38, C5

High on the hill inside the old Fort St School (1856), the SH Ervin Gallery, though surrounded by freeway, is a pleasing oasis that exhibits invariably rewarding historical and contemporary Australian art. Annual mainstays include the Salon des Refusés (alternative Archibald Prize entries) and the Portia Geach Memorial Award. There's a cafe here, too. (📞02-9258 0173; www.shervingallery.com.au; Watson Rd; adult/child $10/free; ⏰11am-5pm Tue-Sun; 🚉Wynyard)

Eating

Fine Food Store   CAFE $

9 ✕ MAP P38, D3

The Rocks sometimes seems all pubs, so it's a delight to find this contemporary cafe that works for a sightseeing stopover or a better, cheaper breakfast than your hotel. Staff are genuinely welcoming, make very respectable coffee and offer delicious panini, sandwiches and other breakfast and lunch fare. The outside tables on this narrow lane are the spot to be. (📞02-9252 1196; www.finefoodstore.com; cnr Mill & Kendall Lanes; light meals $9-16; ⏰7am-4pm Mon-Sat, from 7.30am Sun; 🛜🖊; 🚉Circular Quay)

Barcycle   CAFE $

10 ✕ MAP P38, C3

One of several inviting spots for a light meal on the handsome wharves of Walsh Bay, this hole-in-the-wall is run by a friendly Italian family who offer a range of breakfast and lunch options including 'green eggs' with avocado, pasta, salads and daily specials. The coffee is pretty good, as is the cycling chat: there's an on-site bike workshop here. (📞02-9247 0772; www.barcycle.com.au; Pier 6-7, 19 Hickson Rd; light meals $10-15; ⏰7am-4pm Mon-Sat, to 3pm Sun, later on Fri & Sat evenings in summer; 🛜; 📮324, 325, 🚉Circular Quay)

Quay   MODERN AUSTRALIAN $$$

11 ✕ MAP P38, E3

What many consider to be Sydney's best restaurant matches a peerless bridge view with brilliant food. Chef Peter Gilmore never rests on his laurels, consistently delivering exquisitely crafted, adventurous cuisine. The menu was set to be shaken up in 2018; you can rely on amazing creations.

Book online well in advance, but it's worth phoning in case of cancellations. (📞02-9251 5600; www.quay.com.au; Level 3, Overseas Passenger Terminal; 4/8 courses $180/245; ⏱6-9.30pm Mon-Thu, noon-1.30pm & 6-9.30pm Fri-Sun; 🚇Circular Quay)

Aria

MODERN AUSTRALIAN $$$

12 ❌ MAP P38, F4

Aria is a star in Sydney's fine-dining firmament, an award-winning combination of chef Matt Moran's stellar dishes, floor-to-ceiling windows staring straight

A Gritty Past

After dismissing Botany Bay as a site for the colony, Governor Phillip sailed the First Fleet into what James Cook had named Port Jackson (Warran/Warrane in the local language) and dropped anchor at a horseshoe bay with an all-important freshwater stream running into it. Phillip christened the bay Sydney Cove after the British Home Secretary, Baron Sydney of Chislehurst, who was responsible for the colonies.

The socioeconomic divide of the future city was foreshadowed when the convicts were allocated the rocky land to the west of the stream (known unimaginatively as the Rocks), while the governor and other officials pitched their tents to the east.

Built with convict labour between 1837 and 1844, Circular Quay was originally (and more accurately) called Semicircular Quay, and acted as the main port of Sydney. In the 1850s it was extended further, covering over the by-then festering Tank Stream, which ran into the middle of the cove. As time went on, whalers and sailors joined the ex-convicts at the Rocks – and inns and brothels sprang up to entertain them. With the settlement filthy and overcrowded, the nouveau riche started building houses on the upper slopes, their sewage flowing to the slums below. Residents sloshed through open sewers, and alleys festered with disease and drunken lawlessness. Thus began a long, steady decline.

Bubonic plague broke out in 1900, leading to the razing of entire streets, and Harbour Bridge construction in the 1920s wiped out even more. It wasn't until the 1970s that the Rocks' cultural and architectural heritage was finally recognised.

Much of Millers Point has been public housing for over a century, originally for dock workers. With property prices so high, the State government from 2016 began a series of phases of auctioning off these homes to the highest bidder, evicting one of Sydney's oldest communities in the process and ignoring significant public protest.

Bennelong

Bennelong was born around 1764 into the Wangal tribe, the westerly neighbours of the Gadigal (Cadigal) who lived around central Sydney. Captured in 1789, he was brought to Governor Arthur Phillip, who hoped to use Bennelong to understand the local Aboriginal Australians' customs and language.

Bennelong took to life with the settlers, developing a taste for British food and alcohol, and learning to speak the language of his new 'masters'. Eventually he escaped, but he returned by 1791 when reassured that he would not be held against his will. He developed a strong friendship with Governor Phillip, who had a brick hut built for him on what is now Bennelong Point.

The relationship between Phillip and Bennelong was a fascinating one, and included the governor being speared by an associate of Bennelong while visiting a beached sperm whale at Manly Cove. It may be that it was a kind of ritual payback; Phillip took no retaliation.

In 1792 Bennelong went on a 'civilising' trip to England, and returned in 1795 with a changed dress sense and altered behaviour. Described as good natured and 'stoutly made', Bennelong ultimately was no longer accepted by Aboriginal society and never really found happiness with his white friends either. He died a broken, dispossessed man in 1813.

at the Opera House, a stylishly renovated interior and faultless service. A pre- and post-theatre à la carte menu is perfect for a special meal before or after a night at the Opera House (one/two/three courses $55/90/110). (☏02-9240 2255; www.ariarestaurant.com; 1 Macquarie St; 2-/3-/4-course dinner $115/145/170, degustation $205; ⏰noon-2.15pm & 5.30-10.30pm Mon-Fri, noon-1.30pm & 5-11pm Sat, noon-1.45pm & 5.30-10pm Sun; ☐Circular Quay)

Gantry MODERN AUSTRALIAN $$$

13 ⊗ MAP P38, D2

Despite all that water, there aren't too many harbourside restaurants in this area. Fortunately, Gantry is excellent. Try a wharfside table and enjoy views of Walsh Bay with a screen to protect you from sun and stickybeaks. The food, impeccably sourced from high-quality Australian producers, is delicious, with some standout fish usually on the menu and good vegetarian options. (☏02-8298 9910; www.thegantry.com.au; Wharf 1, 11 Hickson

Rd; mains $36-42; 🕐6-10pm Mon & Tue, noon-2.30pm & 6-10pm Wed-Sun; 📶🚭; 🚌324, 325, 🚆Circular Quay)

Saké
JAPANESE $$$

14 🍴 MAP P38, D4

Colourful sake barrels and lots of dark wood contribute to the louche glamour of this large, buzzy restaurant. Prop yourself around the open kitchen and snack on delectable popcorn shrimp and maki rolls, or grab a table to tuck into multi-course banquets of contemporary Japanese cuisine. (📞02-9259 5656; www.sakerestaurant.com.au; 12 Argyle St; mains $28-46; 🕐noon-3pm & 5.30-10.30pm Mon-Thu, to 11.30pm Fri & Sat, to 10pm Sun; 🚆Circular Quay)

Cafe Sydney
MODERN AUSTRALIAN $$$

15 🍴 MAP P38, E5

This breezy, spacious restaurant on the roof of the **Customs House** (📞02-9242 8551; www.sydney customshouse.com.au; admission free; 🕐8am-midnight Mon-Fri, from 10am Sat, 11am-5pm Sun) has marvellous harbour and bridge views, an outdoor terrace, a glass ceiling, a cocktail bar and friendly staff who greet you straight out of the lift. Quality seafood dishes dominate. It packs out and is often block-booked, so don't expect to show up and get a table. (📞02-9251 8683; www.cafesydney.com; Level 5, Customs House, 31 Alfred St; mains $37-40; 🕐noon-11pm Mon-Fri, from 5pm Sat, noon-3.30pm Sun; 📶; 🚆Circular Quay)

Drinking

Opera Bar
BAR

16 🍺 MAP P38, G3

Right on the harbour with the Opera House on one side and the bridge on the other, this perfectly positioned terrace manages a very Sydney marriage of the laid-back and the sophisticated. It's an iconic spot for visitors and locals alike. There's live music or DJs most nights and really excellent food, running from oysters to fabulous steaks and fish.

It's a very slick operation… staff even geolocate you to know where to bring the food to. (📞02-9247 1666; www.operabar.com.au; lower concourse, Sydney Opera House; 🕐10.30am-midnight Mon-Thu, to 1am Fri, 9am-1am Sat, to midnight Sun; 📶; 🚆Circular Quay)

Hero of Waterloo
PUB

17 🍺 MAP P38, C3

Enter this rough-hewn 1843 sandstone pub to meet some locals, chat to the Irish bar staff and grab an earful of the swing, folk and Celtic bands (Friday to Sunday). Downstairs is a dungeon where, in days gone by, drinkers would sleep off a heavy night before being shanghaied to the high seas via a tunnel leading to the harbour. (📞02-9252 4553; www.heroofwaterloo.com.au; 81 Lower Fort St; 🕐10am-11.30pm Mon-Wed, 10am-midnight Thu-Sat, 10am-10pm Sun; 🚌311, 🚆Circular Quay)

Glenmore Hotel
PUB

18 MAP P38, D4

Downstairs it's a predictably nice old Rocks pub with great outdoor seating, but head to the rooftop and the views are beyond fabulous: Opera House (after the cruise ship leaves), harbour and city skyline all present and accounted for. It gets rammed up here on the weekends, with DJs and plenty of wine by the glass. The food's decent too. (☏02-9247 4794; www.theglenmore.com.au; 96 Cumberland St; ⏱11am-midnight Sun-Thu, to 1am Fri & Sat; ☎; ☒Circular Quay)

Harts Pub
PUB

19 MAP P38, C5

Pouring an excellent range of Sydney craft beers in a quiet corner near the beginning of the Rocks, this historical building has real character. The dishes are quality pub food, with excellent and generous salads, fish and steaks. At weekends, this is enjoyably quieter than other Rocks boozers. There are a few pleasant outdoor tables with the **Shangri-La** (☏02-9250 6000; www.shangri-la. com; 176 Cumberland St; r $350-600; ⓟⓐ❄☎♒) looming above. (☏02-9251 6030; www.hartspub. com; cnr Essex & Gloucester Sts; ⏱noon-11pm Mon-Wed, 11.30am-midnight Thu, to 1am Fri & Sat, noon-10pm Sun; ☎; ☒Circular Quay)

Lord Nelson Brewery Hotel
BREWERY

20 MAP P38, B3

This atmospheric boozer is one of three claiming to be Sydney's oldest (all using slightly different criteria). The on-site brewery cooks up its own natural ales; a pint of dark, stouty Nelson's Blood is a fine way to partake. Pub food downstairs is tasty and solid; the upstairs brasserie is an attractive space doing fancier food, including good seafood choices. (☏02-9251 4044; www.lordnelsonbrewery.com; 19 Kent St; ⏱11am-11pm Mon-Sat, noon-10pm Sun; ☎; ☐311, ☒Circular Quay)

Theatre Bar at the End of the Wharf
BAR

21 MAP P38, C2

It's a long but atmospheric stroll down this wharf building, looking at photos of Sydney Theatre Company performances as you go, to reach the bar at the end. It's a cracking spot, with a magic view of the Harbour Bridge to enjoy with a drink. Also does lunches from noon to 3pm (mains $18 to $28). (☏02-9250 1761; www.sydneytheatre. com.au; Pier 4, 15 Hickson Rd; ⏱noon-11pm Mon-Sat; ☎; ☐324, 325, ☒Circular Quay)

Argyle
BAR, CLUB

22 MAP P38, D4

This stylish and wildly popular conglomeration of bars is spread through the historic Argyle Stores buildings, including a cobblestone courtyard and atmospheric wooden-floored downstairs bar. The decor ranges from rococo couches to white extruded plastic tables, all offset with kooky chandeliers and moody lighting. During the day the courtyard is a pleasant place for a drink or spot of lunch. (📞02-9247 5500; www.theargylerocks.com; 18 Argyle St; ⏰11am-1am Sun-Wed, to 3am Thu-Sat; 🛜; 🚇Circular Quay)

Hotel Palisade
PUB

23 🚇 MAP P38, B3

This historic and hipster-invigorated Millers Point pub preserves its tea-coloured tiles, faded brick and nostalgia-tinted downstairs bar. On top of the venerable building, however, there's a shiny glass section with super bridge views, pricey drinks and posh tapas-style food. It often fills up or books out, but there's a less glitzy, more comfy perch on the little 4th-floor balcony. (📞02-9018 0123; www.hotelpalisade.com; 35 Bettington St; ⏰noon-midnight Mon-Sat, to 10pm Sun; 🛜; 🚌311, 🚇Circular Quay)

Bulletin Place
COCKTAIL BAR

24 🚇 MAP P38, E5

A discreet entrance on this little street of cafes and bars conceals the staircase up to one of Sydney's most talked-about cocktail bars. Personable, down-to-earth staff shake up great daily creations that are high on zinginess and freshness and low on frippery. It's a small space, so get there early. Cocktails are about 20 bucks each. (www.bulletinplace.com; 10 Bulletin Pl; ⏰4pm-midnight Mon-Wed, to 1am Thu-Sat; 🚇Circular Quay)

Australian Hotel
PUB

25 🚇 MAP P38, D4

With its wide verandah shading lots of outdoor seating, this handsome early 20th-century pub is a favoured pit-stop for a cleansing ale; it was doing microbrewed beer long before it became trendy and has a great selection. The kitchen also does a nice line in gourmet pizzas ($17 to $28), including ever-popular toppings of kangaroo, emu and crocodile. (📞02-9247 2229; www.australianheritagehotel.com; 100 Cumberland St; ⏰11am-midnight; 🛜; 🚇Circular Quay)

Fortune of War
PUB

26 🚇 MAP P38, D4

Operating right here since 1828, this pub was rebuilt in the early 20th century and retains much charm from that era in its characterful bar. It has a solid mix of locals and tourists, and features live music on Thursday, Friday and Saturday nights and weekend afternoons. (📞02-9247 2714; www.fortuneofwar.com.au; 137 George St; ⏰9am-midnight Mon-Wed, to 1am Thu, to 2am Fri & Sat, 10am-midnight Sun; 🚇Circular Quay)

Endeavour Tap Rooms

MICROBREWERY

27 🚇 MAP P38, D4

All corridors and slightly awkward spaces, this heritage building in the heart of the Rocks is now a rather lovely brewpub with restrained 1920s-feel decor. There's some top stuff on tap, including the perfectly balanced Australian IPA and other excellent beers. A menu of meaty, smoky fare is on hand. (📞02-9241 6517; www.taprooms.com.au; 39 Argyle St; ⏱11am-midnight Mon-Sat, to 10pm Sun; 🛜; 🚉Circular Quay)

Entertainment

Sydney Opera House

PERFORMING ARTS

28 ⭐ MAP P38, G3

The glamorous jewel at the heart of Australian performance, Sydney's famous Opera House has five main stages. Opera has star billing, but it's also an important venue for theatre, dance and classical concerts, while big-name bands sometimes rock the forecourt. Ongoing renovation works through to 2021 may disrupt some performances, but essentially the show goes on. (📞02-9250 7777; www.sydneyoperahouse.com; Bennelong Point; 🚉Circular Quay)

Sydney Conservatorium of Music

CLASSICAL MUSIC

29 ⭐ MAP P38, G6

This historic venue showcases the talents of its students and their teachers. Choral, jazz, operatic and chamber concerts happen from March to November; check the website (and Facebook page, which often has more info) for details. There are often free recitals. (📞02-9351 1222; http://music.sydney.edu.au; Conservatorium Rd; 🚉Circular Quay)

Sydney Theatre Company

THEATRE

30 ⭐ MAP P38, C2

Established in 1978, the STC is Sydney theatre's top dog and has played an important part in the careers of many famous Australian actors (especially Cate Blanchett, who was co-artistic director from 2008 to 2013). You can book tours of the company's **Wharf** and **Roslyn Packer Theatres** (📞02-9250 1999; www.roslynpackertheatre.com.au; 22 Hickson Rd; tours $10). Performances are also staged at the Opera House. (STC; 📞02-9250 1777; www.sydneytheatre.com.au; Pier 4, 15 Hickson Rd; ⏱box office 9am-7.30pm Mon, to 8.30pm Tue-Fri, 11am-8.30pm Sat, 2hr before show Sun; 🚌324, 325, 🚉Circular Quay)

OpenAir Cinema

CINEMA

31 ⭐ MAP P38, H6

Right on the harbour, the outdoor three-storey screen here comes with surround-sound, sunsets, skyline and swanky food and wine. Most tickets are purchased in advance – look out for the dates in early December as they go fast – but a limited number go on sale at the door each night at 6.30pm; check the website for details. (☏1300 366 649; www.stgeorge openair.com.au; Mrs Macquaries Rd; tickets $39; ◷Jan & Feb; ☷Circular Quay)

Shopping

Gannon House Gallery   ART

32 🔒 MAP P38, D4

Specialising in contemporary Australian and Aboriginal art, Gannon House purchases works directly from artists and Aboriginal communities. You'll find the work of prominent artists such as Gloria Petyarre here, alongside lesser-known names. There are always some striking and wonderful pieces. (☏02-9251 4474; www.gannonhousegallery.com; 45 Argyle St; ◷10am-6pm; ☷Circular Quay)

Craft NSW   ARTS & CRAFTS

33 🔒 MAP P38, E3

Bringing life and verve to the former Coroner's Court, this craft association gallery is full of beautiful and original creations. It's the perfect spot to pick up a unique gift for someone special. (☏02-9241 5825; www.artsand craftsnsw.com.au; 104 George St; ◷9.30am-5.30pm)

Australian Wine Centre   WINE

34 🔒 MAP P38, E6

This store, with multilingual staff, is packed with quality Australian wine, beer and spirits. Smaller producers are well represented, along with a staggering range of prestigious Penfolds Grange wines and other bottle-aged gems. Service is excellent and international shipping can be arranged. (☏02-9247 2755; www.australianwinecentre. com; 42 Pitt St; ◷10am-7pm Mon & Sun, 9.30am-8pm Tue & Wed, to 9pm Thu-Sat; ☷Circular Quay)

Opal Minded   JEWELLERY

35 🔒 MAP P38, E3

This shop in the Rocks is one of several spots around here where you can stock up on opal, that quintessential piece of Aussie bling. The quality and service are both excellent. (☏02-9247 9885; www.opalminded.com; 55 George St; ◷9am-6.30pm; ☷Circular Quay)

The Rocks Markets   MARKET

36 🔒 MAP P38, D3

Under a long white canopy, the stalls at this market are a focus for tourists, but the excellent handicrafts outweigh the amount of koala tat. Pick up tasty treats at the 'Foodies Market' on Fridays or gifts at the weekends. (www.therocks.com/markets; George St; ◷9am-3pm Fri, 10am-5pm Sat & Sun; ☷Circular Quay)

Worth a Trip 🔭

Harbour Highlights

There's nothing better in Sydney than being out on the harbour, and using local ferry services to do your sightseeing is a great experience. You could visit most of these waterside spots in a busy day of ferry-hopping, but take a full day to see Taronga Zoo in the detail it deserves.

Trip Details

Ferries from Circular Quay, some government-run, some private, visit all these spots, some on a hop-on hop-off basis.

Taronga Zoo

A 12-minute ferry ride from Circular Quay, this bushy harbour hillside **zoo** (☏02-9969 2777; www.taronga. org.au; Bradleys Head Rd, Mosman; adult/child $46/26; ☉9.30am-5pm Sep-Apr, to 4.30pm May-Aug; ☷; ☐238, 247, M30, ☂Taronga Zoo) is full of kangaroos, koalas and other hirsute Australian animals, plus numerous imported guests. The zoo's critters have million-dollar harbour views, but seem blissfully unaware of the privilege. Encouragingly, Taronga sets benchmarks in animal care and welfare. Highlights include the nocturnal platypus habitat, the Great Southern Oceans section and the Asian elephant display. Feedings happen throughout the day.

Catching the ferry is part of the fun. From the wharf, the **Sky Safari** cable car or a bus will whisk you to the entrance, from which you can traverse the zoo downhill back to the ferry.

Luna Park

A sinister clown face (pictured) forms the entrance to this old-fashioned **amusement park** (☏02-9922 6644; www.lunaparksydney.com; 1 Olympic Dr, Milsons Point; admission free; ☉11am-10pm Fri & Sat, 10am-6pm Sun, 11am-4pm Mon; ☂Milsons Point, ☐Milsons Point) overlooking Sydney Harbour. It's one of several 1930s features, including the Coney Island funhouse, a pretty carousel and the nausea-inducing Rotor. You can purchase a two-ride pass ($20), or buy a height-based unlimited-ride pass (adults $52, kids $22 to $42, cheaper online).

McMahons Point

Is there a better view of the Bridge and the Opera House than from the wharf at this **point** (Henry Lawson Ave; ☂McMahons Point)? Only a short hop by ferry northwest of the city centre, the vista is all unfolded before you: it's a stunning spot to be when the sun is setting.

Garden Island

The majority of this naval base is off-limits, but you can visit the tip by ferry. There's a pleasant garden and lookout as well as a cafe and a **naval museum** (☏02-9359 2003; www.navy.gov.au; admission free; ☉9.30am-3.30pm; ☂Garden Island). It's a modern display with wartime paraphernalia, weapons, submarine control consoles and a periscope you can use to observe the harbour.

Fort Denison

In colonial times this small **island** (☏restaurant 02-9361 5208, tour bookings 1300 72757; www.fortdenison. au; tour plus ferry adult/child $37.50/29; ☉tours 11.15am, 12.15pm, 2pm & 3.10pm; ☂Fort Denison) was used to isolate convicts and nicknamed 'Pinchgut' for its meagre rations. Fears of Russian invasion during the Crimean War led to its fortification. The **NPWS** (☏1300 072757; www.nationalparks.nsw.gov.au) offers tours of the tower (prebook online), although many people just pop over for lunch at the outdoor restaurant.

Worth a Trip 🔭

Upriver to Parramatta

Sydney Harbour gets all the attention, but a jaunt upriver is just as interesting. As you pass old industrial sites and the Olympic complex, or gaze into millionaires' backyards, a window opens onto a watery world in the heart of Sydney. Parramatta combines treasures from the earliest days of European colonization with ambitious modern development.

Trip Details

The F3 ferry line runs from Circular Quay to Parramatta (1¼ hours) via Cockatoo Island (also served by F8 ferries). It's faster but less scenic to reach Parramatta by train.

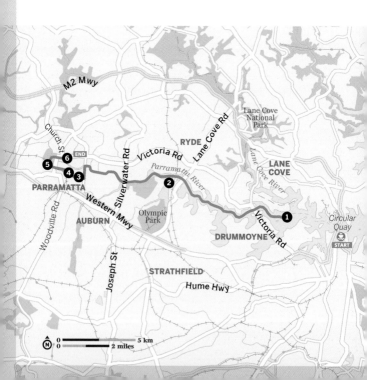

❶ Explore Cockatoo Island

Ferry from Circular Quay to fascinating **Cockatoo Island** (☎02-8969 2100; www.cockatooisland.gov.au; ⚓Cockatoo Island). Studded with industrial relics, convict architecture and art, it opened to the public in 2007. Information boards and audio guides ($5) explain the island's various uses as a prison, a shipyard and a naval base. A spooky tunnel passes clear through the middle.

❷ Up the River

Catch the F3 ferry from Cockatoo Island upriver towards Parramatta. You'll pass 640-hectare **Sydney Olympic Park** before disembarking at **Parramatta**, founded in 1788 by Governor Phillip, who needed a place to grow grain to supply the colony. Big things are afoot in Parramatta, which is undergoing a massive and ambitious development program.

❸ Elizabeth Farm

Walk east from the ferry stop to **Elizabeth Farm** (☎02-9635 9488; www.sydneylivingmuseums.com.au; 70 Alice St, Rosehill; adult/child $12/8; ⊗10am-4pm Wed-Sun; ⚓Rosehill, ⚓Harris Park when Rosehill is closed), which contains part of Australia's oldest surviving colonial building (1793), built by pastoralist and rum trader John Macarthur. The homestead is now a hands-on museum where you can sit on the reproduction furniture and read Elizabeth Macarthur's letters.

❹ Experiment Farm Cottage

Near Elizabeth Farm, this **colonial bungalow** (☎02-9635 5655; www.nationaltrust.org.au; 9 Ruse St, Harris Park; adult/child $9/4; ⊗guided tours 10.30am-3.30pm Wed-Sun; ⚓Harris Park) stands on the site of Australia's first official land grant in 1789. The house, built around 1835, is decked out in period style with lovely early-colonial furniture. Entrance is by an informative guided tour.

❺ Old Government House

Walk through the rapidly-changing centre of Parramatta to Parramatta Park, a lovely riverside spot containing **Old Government House** (☎02-9635 8149; www.nationaltrust.org.au; Parramatta Park, Parramatta; adult/child $14/6; ⊗10am-4pm Tue-Sun; ⚓Parramatta), the oldest remaining public building in Australia (1799). Temporary exhibitions add to the building's interest and there's a vine-draped courtyard restaurant.

❻ A Riverside Stroll

Cross the bridge across the river and head back east along the **bankside path**. It's a lovely stroll that will take you back to the ferry, where you can sip a drink at the adjacent bar/restaurant while you wait. If you want to get back to town more quickly, head for Parramatta train station instead.

Explore ⬡
City Centre
& Haymarket

Occupying a rough grid pattern south of the Rocks, Sydney's central business district (CBD) offers upmarket shopping, eating and sightseeing, with gracious colonial buildings scattered among the skyscrapers and orderly parks providing breathing space. The breathless jumble of Haymarket and Chinatown provides a chaotic contrast.

Sydney's towering central business district (CBD) encapsulates the city's cavalier spirit, with skyscrapers unashamedly overshadowing historic sandstone buildings and churches.

While pacing the grid of central streets gives a good idea of contemporary corporate Sydney, it's worth identifying a few key spots of interest before plunging into the urban jungle. Make sure to dedicate a little time to strolling Hyde Park and the array of historic buildings along Macquarie Street.

Getting There & Around

🚈 Train is the best option for getting here, with six stations.

🚌 There are numerous bus lines, with major nodes at Wynyard Park, the QVB and Central station (Railway Sq).

🚊 One light-rail line from Glebe and Pyrmont. From 2019 another will run the length of the CBD along George St, from Circular Quay to Central before heading out to the southeast.

City Centre & Haymarket Map on p62

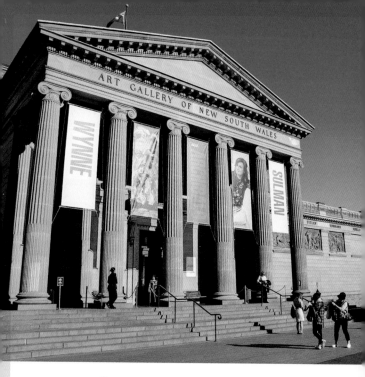

Top Sight 📷
Art Gallery of NSW

The city's major gallery is a cornerstone of Sydney life. While locals throng to the major touring exhibitions, the main attraction here is the outstanding assemblage of Indigenous and colonial Australian art. There's also a lively line-up of cultural events and children's activities. An expansion is due to add a modern annex, Sydney Modern, scheduled for completion in 2021.

◎ **MAP P62, F3**

☎ 1800 679 278

www.artgallery.nsw.gov.au

Art Gallery Rd

admission free

⏱ 10am-5pm Thu-Tue, to 10pm Wed

🚌 441, 🚉 St James

The Collection

While the permanent collection has a strong collection of 19th-century European and Australian art, the highlights are the contemporary Indigenous gallery in the basement, and the collection of 20th-century Australian art, with some standout canvases by the big names of the local painting scene. Look out for Albert Tucker's scary *Apocalyptic Horse*, Russell Drysdale's brilliant gold-town street *Sofala* and half a room of Sidney Nolans, usually including one or more of his extraordinary Ned Kelly paintings. There's a good representation of female artists too, including Grace Cossington Smith and several Margaret Olleys on rotation. Arthur Boyd works include his terracotta sculpture of *Judas Kissing Christ*, while Brett Whiteley is represented by the intoxicatingly blue harbour of *The Balcony 2*.

Prizes

The $100,000 **Archibald Prize** for portraiture is a much-talked-about Sydney event that garners attention with its lure of celebrity subjects. It's so popular that it's generated three spin-offs: the Salon des Refusés at the SH Ervin Gallery (p42); the highly irreverent Bald Archies; and the Packing Room Prize (judged by the employees who unload the crates).

The $50,000 **Wynne Prize** for landscape painting or figure sculpture and the $40,000 **Sir John Sulman Prize** for subject or mural painting don't usually cause as much consternation.

New Developments

Construction of a second building was approved in 2017 and is due to be completed in 2021. Occupying space to the north of the existing building, it's a major project, to be known as Sydney Modern, that will be centred around a new Indigenous gallery and a dedicated space for major touring exhibitions. The construction work shouldn't affect gallery visits.

★ Top Tips

○ Major exhibitions absolutely pack out at weekends, so try and visit midweek if Picasso or Van Gogh are in town.

○ Check the gallery website before you visit, as all sorts of activities and events are often on.

✕ Take a Break

The gallery's **restaurant** (☏ 02-9225 1819; www.chiswick restaurant.com.au; Art Gallery Rd; small plates $19-25, mains $29-40; ⊙ noon-3.30pm Thu-Tue, to 9pm Wed; 🐶), on the entrance level, and **cafe**, a floor down, are pleasant spaces with outdoor seating and harbour views.

Wander down to Woolloomooloo Bay for a pie at Harry's Cafe de Wheels (p136) or upmarket harbourside Italian at Otto (p139).

Top Sight 📷
Chinatown

Wedged into the Haymarket district, Sydney's Chinatown is a tight nest of restaurants, food courts, shops and aroma-filled alleyways, centred on Dixon St. No longer just Chinese, the area is truly pan-Asian. Head here for cheap eats any time of the day or night.

◎ **MAP P62, B7**

www.sydney-chinatown.info

🚊 Paddy's Markets,
🚊 Town Hall

Dixon Street

Dixon St is the heart of Chinatown: a narrow, shady pedestrian mall with a string of restaurants and insistent spruikers. The ornate dragon gates (*paifang*) at either end have fake bamboo tiles, golden Chinese calligraphy and ornamental lions to keep evil spirits at bay.

This is actually Sydney's third Chinatown: the first was in the Rocks in the late 19th century before it moved to the Darling Harbour end of Market St. Dixon St's Chinatown dates from the 1920s. Look for the fake-bamboo awnings guarded by dragons, dogs and lions, and kooky upturned-wok lighting fixtures.

Other Areas

On Chinatown's western border, the Chinese Garden of Friendship (pictured; p79) is a peaceful oasis, while on Hay St, the Golden Water Mouth sculpture represents a symbolic fusion of China and Australia. A little further down Hay St, Paddy's Markets (p75) fills the lower level of a hefty brick building. It started out in the mid-19th century with mainly European traders, but these days the tightly packed market stalls are more evocative of present-day Vietnam.

Eating

Chinatown in general (not necessarily just between the dragon gates) is a fabulous eating district, which effectively extends for several blocks north and south of Dixon Street. Beyond Paddy's Markets, there's some great cheap eating to be done in the area around Thomas and Quay Streets and Ultimo Road. To the east, across George Street, Chinatown segues into Koreatown and Thaitown, with more great eateries.

★ **Top Tips**

o It's worth visiting twice: once during the day to see the bustle of the markets and shops, and again after dark for the all-night buzz.

o Though it's got the dragon gates, Dixon Street is arguably the least interesting part of Chinatown: make sure you explore further.

✗ **Take a Break**

The area's food courts hide numerous quality noodle outlets. Gumshara (p67) does legendary ramen.

For a traditional and upmarket Chinese dining experience, check in to Golden Century (p71). Order seafood.

Walking Tour

City Escapes

Sydney's two most imposing streets are Macquarie St, the centre of government, and intersecting with it, Martin Place, its financial heart. During weekdays they thrum to the beat of politics and commerce. When the daily hustle gets too much, bureaucrats and office workers seek sanctuary in the inner city's parks or head to Pitt Street Mall for some shopfront fantasies.

Walk Facts

Start The Domain
End Hyde Park
Length 2.5km, one to two hours

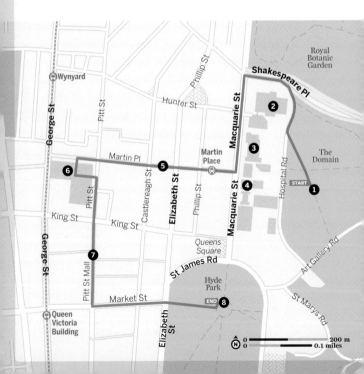

① Dawdle Through the Domain

This large **grassy tract** (www.rbgsyd. nsw.gov.au; Art Gallery Rd; [R] St James) was set aside by Governor Phillip in 1788 for public recreation. Today's city workers use the space to work up a sweat or eat their lunch. Large-scale public events are also held here.

② Study the State Library

Scholars sneak off to the elegant main reading room of the **State Library of NSW** ([J] 02-9273 1414; www.sl.nsw.gov.au; Macquarie St; admission free; ⊙9am-8pm Mon-Thu, to 5pm Fri, 10am-5pm Sat & Sun; [R] Martin Place) seeking inspiration within its milky marble walls. The library holds more than five million tomes and good temporary exhibitions.

③ Visit the People's Place

Built in 1816 as part of the Rum Hospital, **Parliament House** ([J] 02-9230 2111; www.parliament. nsw.gov.au; 6 Macquarie St; admission free; ⊙9am-5pm Mon-Fri; [R] Martin Place) has been home to the Parliament of New South Wales since 1829, making it the world's oldest continually operating parliament building. Everyone's welcome to visit the assembly chambers, art exhibitions and historical displays.

④ Sydney Hospital

Australia's oldest **hospital** (8 Macquarie St; [R] Martin Place) has a grand Victorian sandstone facade and a peaceful central courtyard with a cafe. In provocative recline out the front of the hospital is the pig-ugly bronze statue Il Porcellino. Rub its snout for luck.

⑤ March Down Martin Place

Studded with imposing edifices, **Martin Place** ([R] Wynyard, [R] Martin Place) was closed to traffic in 1971, forming a pedestrian mall. It's the closest thing to a town square that Sydney has. Near the George St end is the Cenotaph, commemorating Australia's war dead.

⑥ Rehydrate in GPO Sydney

As iconic as the Opera House in its time (1874), the **General Post Office** (GPO; www.gpogrand.com; 1 Martin Pl; [R] Wynyard, [R] Martin Place), a colonnaded Victorian palazzo, has been gutted, stabbed with office towers and transformed into a hotel, restaurants and bars.

⑦ Pitt Street Mall Shopping

As you sidestep the buskers on this car-free shopping street, look out for the Strand Arcade on your right and Westfield Sydney on your left.

⑧ Hang Out in Hyde Park

Formal but much-loved **Hyde Park** (Elizabeth St; [R] St James, Museum) has manicured gardens and a tree-formed tunnel running down its spine. The park's northern end is crowned by the richly symbolic art deco **Archibald Memorial Fountain**, featuring Greek mythological figures, while at the other end is the **Anzac Memorial**.

City Centre & Haymarket

For reviews see	
○ Top Sights	p56
⊙ Sights	p64
⊗ Eating	p67
⊕ Drinking	p71
⊕ Entertainment	p73
⊕ Shopping	p74

City Centre & Haymarket

Eastbound Cross City Tunnel
Westbound Cross City Tunnel

Bourke St
Palmer St
Crown St
Stanley St
Riley St
Seale St
Yurong St
Francis St
College St
Liverpool St
Oxford St
Burton St
Foley St
Langley St
Taylor Square
Flinders St
Campbell St
Crown St
Riley St
EAST SYDNEY
Park St
Pool of Reflection
Anzac Memorial
Museum
Waine St
Brisbane St
Wentworth Ave
Nithsdale St
Harmony Park
Hunt St
Campbell St
Smith St
Batman La
SURRY HILLS
Ann St
Mary St
Foster St
Reservoir St
Albion St
Foy La
Elizabeth St
400 m
0.2 miles
N
E
D
F

Elizabeth St
Castlereagh St
Bathurst St
Pitt St
Central St
City Host Information Kiosk
Town Hall
Liverpool St
Goulburn St
World Square
Chinatown
Campbell St
Capitol Square
HAYMARKET
Rawson Place
Belmore Park
Eddy Ave
Central
Elizabeth St
17
35
16
41

Town Hall
Bathurst St
Kent St
Sussex St
Harbour St
Dixon St
Goulburn St
Pier St
Chinese Garden of Friendship
City Host Information Kiosk
Chinatown
Paddy's Markets
Thomas St
Quay St
Ultimo Rd
Darling Dr
Harris St
UTS
George St
Pitt St
George St
21
11
23

DARLING HARBOUR
Western Distributor
Tumbalong Park

A B C

Sights

Queen Victoria Building
HISTORIC BUILDING

1 MAP P62, C4

Unbelievably, this High Victorian Gothic masterpiece (1898) was repeatedly slated for demolition before it was restored in the 1980s. Occupying an entire city block on the site of the city's first markets, it is a Venetian Romanesque–inspired temple to the gods of retail. (QVB; ☎02-9264 9209; www.qvb.com.au; 455 George St; tours $15; ⏰9am-6pm Mon-Wed, Fri & Sat, 9am-9pm Thu, 11am-5pm Sun; 🚇Town Hall)

Sydney Tower Eye
TOWER

2 MAP P62, C4

The 309m-tall Sydney Tower (finished in 1981 and still known as Centrepoint by many Sydneysiders) offers unbeatable 360-degree views from the observation level 250m up – and even better ones for the daredevils braving the Skywalk on its roof. The visit starts with the 4D Experience, a short 3D film giving you a bird's-eye view (a parakeet's to be exact) of city, surf, harbour and what lies beneath the water, accompanied by mist sprays and bubbles – it's actually pretty darn cool.

Luke Skywalker aspirations? Don a spiffy 'skysuit' and take the **Skywalk**: shackle yourself to the safety rail and step onto two glass-floored viewing platforms outside Sydney Tower's observation deck, 268m above the street. It's no place for the weak-bowelled. Tickets are cheaper online, or as part of a Sydney Attractions Pass. The entrance is on the 5th floor of the **Westfield shopping centre** (☎02-8236 9200; www.westfield.com.au/sydney; ⏰9.30am-7pm Mon-Wed, Fri & Sat, to 9pm Thu, 10am-7pm Sun; 📶), near the food court but surprisingly poorly signposted. There are two revolving restaurants: an extremely mediocre buffet and a somewhat better fine-dining establishment. In the revolving dining stakes, O Bar (p73) in the Australia Square building is a better bet. (www.sydneytowereye.com.au; Level 5, Westfield Sydney, 188 Pitt St; adult/child $28/19, Skywalk $70/49; ⏰9am-9.30pm May-Sep, to 10pm Oct-Apr; 🚇St James)

Hyde Park Barracks Museum
MUSEUM

3 MAP P62, E3

Convict architect Francis Greenway designed this squarish, decorously Georgian structure (1819) as convict quarters. Fifty thousand men and boys sentenced to transportation passed through here in 30 years. It later became an immigration depot, a women's asylum and a law court. These days it's a fascinating museum, focusing on the barracks' history and the archaeological efforts that helped reveal it. The top floor has hammocks strung out as they were back in the day. Entry includes a good audio guide. (☎02-8239 2311; www.sydneylivingmuseums.com.au; Queens Sq, Macquarie St; adult/child $12/8; ⏰10am-5pm; 🚇St James)

Museum of Sydney

MUSEUM

4 ⊙ MAP P62, D1

Built on the site of Sydney's first Government House, the MoS is a fragmented, storytelling museum, which uses installations to explore the city's history. The area's long Indigenous past is highlighted, plus there's interesting coverage of the early days of contact between the Gadigal (Cadigal) people and the colonists. Key figures in Sydney's planning and architecture are brought to life, while there's a good section on the First Fleet itself, with scale models. (MoS; ☎02-9251 5988; www.sydneylivingmuseums.com.au; cnr Phillip & Bridge Sts; adult/child $12/8; ⏲10am-5pm; ☒Circular Quay)

St Mary's Cathedral

CHURCH

5 ⊙ MAP P62, E4

Sydney has traditionally been quite a Catholic city, and this is the hub of the faith. Built to last, this 106m-long sandstone Gothic Revival–style cathedral was begun in 1868, consecrated in 1905 and substantially finished in 1928, though the massive, 75m-high spires weren't added until 2000. The **crypt** ($5 admission, 10am to 4pm weekdays) has bishops' tombs and an impressive cross-shaped terrazzo mosaic floor depicting the Creation, inspired by the Celtic-style illuminations of the *Book of Kells*. (☎02-9220 0400; www.stmaryscathedral.org.au; St Marys Rd; ⏲6.30am-6.30pm; ☒St James)

Sydney Tower Eye

Anzac Memorial

MEMORIAL

6 MAP P62, D6

Fronted by the Pool of Reflection, this dignified art-deco memorial (1934) commemorates the soldiers of the Australia and New Zealand Army Corps (Anzacs) who served in WWI. The interior dome is studded with 120,000 stars: one for each New South Welsh soldier who served. These twinkle above Rayner Hoff's poignant sculpture *Sacrifice.* Scheduled for completion in late 2018 is a new Hall of Service, to feature names and soil samples of all the NSW places of origin of WWI soldiers. (☎02-9267 7668; www.anzacmemorial.nsw.gov.au; Hyde Park; admission free; ⏱9am-5pm; 🚇Museum)

St James' Church

CHURCH

7 MAP P62, D3

Built from convict-made bricks, Sydney's oldest church (1819) is widely considered to be architect Francis Greenway's masterpiece. It was originally designed as a courthouse, but the brief changed and the cells became the crypt. Check out the dark-wood choir loft, the sparkling copper dome, the crypt and the 1950s stained-glass 'Creation Window'. It's worth reading the marble plaques along the walls for some insights into early colonial life and exploration. A more recent plaque commemorates Gough and Margaret Whitlam. (☎02-8227 1300; www.sjks.org.au; 173 King St; ⏱10am-4pm Mon-Fri, to 1pm Sat, 7.30am-2pm Sun; 🚇St James)

Sydney Town Hall

HISTORIC BUILDING

8 MAP P62, C5

Mansard roofs, sandstone turrets, wrought-iron trimmings and over-the-top balustrades: the French Second Empire wedding-cake exterior of the Town Hall (built 1868–89) is something to behold. Unless there's something on, you can poke your head into an ornate hall inside; for further access you'll need to take the two-hour **guided tour** ($5, Tuesdays 10.30am). The wood-lined concert hall has a **giant organ** with nearly 9000 pipes, once the largest in the world. It's used regularly for recitals, some of which are free. (www.sydneytownhall. com.au; 483 George St; ⏱8am-6pm Mon-Fri; 🚇Town Hall)

The Mint

HISTORIC BUILDING

9 MAP P62, D3

The stately Mint building (1816) was originally the southern wing of the infamous Rum Hospital (p61), built by two Sydney merchants in return for a monopoly on the rum trade (Sydney's currency in those days). It became a branch of the Royal Mint in 1854, the first outside England. It's now head office for the Historic Houses Trust. Beyond the upstairs restaurant and a boutique downstairs, there's not a whole lot to see or do, but it's a worthwhile diversion nonetheless. (☎02-8239 2288; www.sydneylivingmuseums.com. au; 10 Macquarie St; admission free; ⏱9am-5pm Mon-Fri; 🚇St James)

Great Synagogue

SYNAGOGUE

10 ◉ MAP P62, D4

The heritage-listed Great Synagogue (1878) is the spiritual home of Sydney's oldest Jewish congregation, established in 1831. It's considered the Mother Synagogue of Australia and is architecturally the most important in the southern hemisphere, combining Romanesque, Gothic, Moorish and Byzantine elements. Tours include the **AM Rosenblum Museum** artefacts and a video presentation on Jewish beliefs, traditions and history in Australia. (☏02-9267 2477; www.greatsynagogue.org.au; 187a Elizabeth St; tours adult/child $10/5; ⏱tours noon Thu & 1st & 3rd Tue; ☒St James)

Eating

Gumshara

RAMEN $

11 ✖ MAP P62, B6

Prepare to queue for some of Sydney's best broth at this convivial ramen house in a popular Chinatown budget-price food court. They boil down over 100kg of pork bones for a week to make the gloriously thick and sticky liquid. There are lots of options, including some that pack quite a punch. Ask for extra back fat for real indulgence. (☏0410 253 280; Shop 211, 25-29 Dixon St; ramen $12-19; ⏱11.30am-9pm Tue-Sat, to 8.30pm Sun & Mon; ☒Paddy's Markets, ☒Central)

Restaurant Hubert

FRENCH $$

12 ✖ MAP P62, D1

The memorable descent into the sexy old-time ambience plunges you straight from suity Sydney to some 1930s cocktail movie. Delicious French fare comes in old-fashioned portions – think terrine, black pudding or duck, plus a few more avant-garde creations. Candlelit tables and a long whisky-backed counter provide seating. No bookings for small groups, so wait it out in the bar area.

This is one of the few top-quality venues in Sydney to serve food this late. The bar in itself makes a great destination for a few cocktails – check out the vast collection of miniature bottles on your way down. (☏02-9232 0881; www.restauranthubert.com; 15 Bligh St; mains $15-48; ⏱noon-3pm & 5pm-1am Mon-Fri, 5pm-1am Sat; ☒Martin Place)

Pablo & Rusty's

CAFE $$

13 ✖ MAP P62, C4

Busy and loud, with close-packed tables, this excellent cafe is high-energy. The inviting wood-and-brick decor and seriously good coffee (several single-origins available daily) is complemented by a range of appealing breakfast and lunch specials ranging from large sourdough sandwiches to wholesome Mediterranean- and Asian-influenced combos such as tuna poke with brown rice or lychee and ginger tapioca. (☏02-9283 9543; www.pabloandrustys.com.au; 161 Castlereagh St; light meals $9-25;

6.30am-5pm Mon-Fri, 8am-3pm Sat;
; Town Hall)

Mr Wong
CHINESE $$

14 MAP P62, C1

Classy but comfortable in an attractive, low-lit space on a CBD laneway, this has exposed-brick colonial warehouse chic and a huge team of staff and hanging ducks in the open kitchen. Lunchtime dim sum offerings bristle with flavour and the salad offerings are mouth-freshening sensations. Mains such as crispy pork hock are sinfully sticky, while Peking duck rolls are legendary.

An impressive wine list and attentive, sassy service seals the deal. (02-9240 3000; www.merivale.

com.au/mrwong; 3 Bridge Lane; mains $22-40; lunch noon-3pm Mon-Fri, 10.30am-3pm Sat & Sun, dinner 5.30-11pm Mon-Wed, to midnight Thu-Sat, to 10pm Sun; ; Wynyard)

Grounds of the City
CAFE $$

15 MAP P62, C4

Peddling everything from takeaway snacks and scientifically roasted coffee to fuller meals and cocktails in a striking curiosity-shop interior, this scion of its Alexandria (p95) parent represents a significant hipster conquest of the somewhat staid CBD fortress. There's an amazing range of eating and drinking, from fresh-baked breakfast rolls to flower-strewn gin concoctions and delights wheeled around on the dessert trolley. (02-9699 2235; www.thegroundscity.com.au; 500 George St; lunch mains $20-35; 7am-5pm Mon, to 9.30pm Tue-Thu, to 10pm Fri, 8am-10pm Sat, 8am-9.30pm Sun; ; Town Hall)

Chat Thai
THAI $$

16 MAP P62, C7

Cooler than your average Thai joint, this Thaitown linchpin is so popular that a list is posted outside for you to affix your name to should you want a table. Expat Thais flock here for the dishes that don't make it onto your average suburban Thai restaurant menu – particularly the more unusual sweets. (02-9211 1808; www.chat thai.com.au; 20 Campbell St; mains $13-25; 10am-2am; ; Capitol Square, Central)

Yum Cha

Despite the larger restaurants seating hundreds of dumpling devotees, there always seem to be queues in Chinatown on weekend mornings for yum cha. Literally meaning 'drink tea', it's really an opportunity to gorge on small plates of dim sum, wheeled between the tables on trolleys. Popular places for traditional fare include Marigold (www.marigold.com. au, 683 George St) and Golden Century (p71). Outside the district, Bodhi (p69) is great for vegans, while Mr Wong (p68) puts a contemporary twist on the dishes.

Yum cha

Sydney Madang KOREAN $$

17 MAP P62, C6

Down a teensy Little Korea lane is this backdoor gem – an authentic BBQ joint that's low on interior charisma but high on quality and quantity. Noisy, cramped and chaotic, yes, but the chilli seafood soup will have you coming back. Try the delicious cold noodles, too. Prepare to queue at weekends. (02-9264 7010; 371a Pitt St; mains $14-28; 11.30am-2am; Museum)

Bodhi VEGAN, ASIAN $$

18 MAP P62, E4

Bodhi scores highly for its cool design and leafy position near St Mary's Cathedral. With its pretty outdoor area, it's a relaxing Asian haven from CBD stress. Vegan yum cha is served until 4pm, switching to 'Oriental tapas' and more substantial plates until close. The barbecue buns rule. (02-9360 2523; www.bodhirestaurant.com.au; Cook + Phillip Park, 2-4 College St; dishes lunch $9-10, dinner mains $23-30; 11am-4pm Mon, to 10pm Tue-Sun; ; St James)

Azuma JAPANESE $$$

19 MAP P62, D2

Tucked away upstairs in Chifley Plaza, this is one of Sydney's finest Japanese restaurants. Sushi and sashimi are of stellar quality and too pretty to eat – almost. Other options include sukiyaki and hot-pot DIY dishes and excellent tasting menus. It's a great place to get acquainted with high-class modern Japanese fare.

Food Courts

Though they aren't necessarily visible from the street, Sydney's CBD is absolutely riddled with food courts, which can be great places for a budget meal, especially at lunchtime. Look for them in shopping centres and major office towers. Some worthwhile ones are in Westfield Sydney, in Australia Square, at the north end underground in the QVB, between George and Pitt Sts north of Liverpool St, in World Square and in the Sussex Centre.

Sushi places in particular tend to start discounting in the mid-afternoon; Friday afternoons see a big sell-off at CBD food courts.

It also has some moreish sake by the carafe. (☎02-9222 9960; www.azuma.com.au; Level 1, Chifley Plaza, Hunter St; mains $29-39, tasting menus $70-110; ☺noon-2.30pm & 6-10pm Mon-Fri, 6-10pm Sat; ♒Martin Place)

Rockpool Bar & Grill   STEAK $$$

21 ✖ MAP P62, D2

You'll feel like a 1930s Manhattan stockbroker when you dine at this sleek operation in the fabulous art-deco City Mutual Building. The bar is famous for its dry-aged, full-blood Wagyu burger (make sure you order a side of the hand-cut fat chips), but carnivores will be equally enamoured with the succulent steaks, stews and fish dishes served in the grill. (☎02-8078 1900; www.rockpoolbarandgrill.com.au; 66 Hunter St; mains $35-65, bar mains $19-35; ☺noon-3pm & 6-11pm Mon-Fri, 5.30-11pm Sat, 6-10pm Sun; ♒Martin Place)

Tetsuya's   FRENCH, JAPANESE $$$

21 ✖ MAP P62, B5

Concealed in a villa behind a historic cottage amid the high-rises, this extraordinary restaurant is for those seeking a culinary journey rather than a simple stuffed belly. Settle in for 10-plus courses of French- and Japanese-inflected food from the genius of legendary Sydney chef Tetsuya Wakuda. It's all great, but the seafood is sublime. Great wine list. Book well ahead. (☎02-9267 2900; www.tetsuyas.com; 529 Kent St; degustation menu $230, matching wines $125; ☺5.30-10pm Tue-Fri, noon-3pm & 5.30-10pm Sat; ♒Town Hall)

Bentley Restaurant & Bar   MODERN AUSTRALIAN $$$

22 ✖ MAP P62, C2

Its chic corporate veneer blending plush with industrial, Bentley has been turning heads in Sydney for the sheer quality of its imaginative dishes. Many of these have a distinctly Australian taste, with native fruits and seeds lending their unusual flavours. The bar is also a good spot to hang out, with pricey but delicious share plates of similar fare. (☎02-8214 0505; www.thebentley.com.au; cnr Pitt & Hunter Sts; mains $46-70, tasting menus $120-150; ⏰noon-3pm & 6pm-midnight Mon-Fri, 6pm-midnight Sat; 🛜🎫; 🚇Wynyard)

Golden Century

CHINESE, SEAFOOD $$$

23 🍴 MAP P62, B6

The fish tank at this frenetic Cantonese place, a Chinatown classic, forms a window-wall to the street, filled with fish, crabs, lobsters and abalone. Splash out on the whole lobster cooked in ginger and shallots or try the delicious beef brisket with turnips. It's open very late but is also wildly popular for weekend yum cha. (☎02-9212 3901; www. goldencentury.com.au; 393-399 Sussex St; mains $25-43; ⏰noon-4am; 🎫; 🚇Town Hall)

Drinking

Uncle Ming's

COCKTAIL BAR

24 🍺 MAP P62, B2

We love the dark romantic opium-den atmosphere of this small bar secreted away in a basement by a shirt shop. It's an atmospheric spot for anything from a quick beer before jumping on a train at Wynyard to a leisurely exploration of the cocktail menu. It also does an excellent line in dumplings and, usually, has very welcoming bar staff. (www.unclemings.com.au; 55 York St; ⏰noon-midnight Mon-Fri, 4pm-midnight Sat; 🚇Wynyard)

Frankie's Pizza

BAR

25 🍺 MAP P62, D2

Descend the stairs and you'll think you're in a 1970s pizzeria, complete with plastic grapevines, snapshots covering the walls and tasty pizza slices ($6). But open the nondescript door in the corner and an indie wonder-land reveals itself. Bands play here at least four nights a week (join them on Tuesdays for live karaoke) and there's another bar hidden below. (www.frankies pizzabytheslice.com; 50 Hunter St; ⏰4pm-3am Sat-Thu, noon-3am Fri; 🛜; 🚇Martin Place)

Baxter Inn

BAR

26 🍺 MAP P62, B3

Yes, it really is down that dark lane and through that unmarked door (there are two easily-spotted bars on this courtyard, but this is through a door to your right). Whisky's the main poison and the friendly bar staff really know their stuff. There's an elegant speakeasy atmosphere and a mighty impressive choir of bottles behind the bar. (www.thebaxterinn.com; 152-156 Clarence St; ⏰4pm-1am Mon-Sat; 🚇Town Hall)

Ivy

BAR, CLUB

27 🍺 MAP P62, C2

Hidden down a lane off George St, Ivy is the HQ of the all-pervading Merivale Group. It's a fashionable complex of bars, restaurants... even a swimming pool. It's also

Sydney's most hyped venue; expect lengthy queues of suburban kids teetering on high heels, waiting to shed $40 on a Saturday for Sydney's hottest club nights, run by Ministry of Sound. (☎02-9254 8100; www.merivale.com/ivy; Level 1, 330 George St; ⏱noon-midnight Mon-Fri, 8.30pm-3.30am Sat, plus pool party 1pm-midnight Sun Oct-Mar; 🛜; 🚆Wynyard)

Slip Inn & Chinese Laundry

PUB, CLUB

28 🚇 MAP P62, B3

Slip in to this cheerfully colourful atmospheric warren on the edge of Darling Harbour and bump hips with the kids. There are bars, pool tables, a beer garden and Mexican food, courtesy of El Loco. On Friday and Saturday nights the bass cranks up at the long-running attached Chinese Laundry nightclub, accessed via Slip St below. (☎02-9254 8088; www.merivale.

Small Bars

Though the CBD can be a bit lacking in atmosphere at night, once the office workers have gone home, there's more going on than first meets the eye. An array of 'small bars' are tucked away in hard-to-guess locations around the area. You can fashion a rewarding cocktail crawl of them...if you can find the way in.

---

com.au/chineselaundry; 111 Sussex St; club $28-33; ⏱11am-1am Mon-Thu, to 3am Fri, 2pm-3am Sat, Chinese Laundry 9pm-3.30am Fri & Sat; 🛜; 🚆Wynyard)

Barber Shop

COCKTAIL BAR

29 🚇 MAP P62, B3

No, it's not a themed bar but a real barber. Walk on past the blokes getting a short-back-and-sides and you'll find a seductive spot peddling gin, cocktails and quality beers. The courtyard space out the back is great for a mingle on a hot summer night. You can also enter from Clarence St, down the laneway between 152 and 156. (☎02-9299 9699; www.thisisthe barbershop.com; 89 York St; ⏱4pm-midnight Mon-Wed & Sat, 3pm-midnight Thu & Fri; 🛜; 🚆Town Hall)

Palmer & Co

BAR

30 🚇 MAP P62, C1

A self-consciously hip member of Sydney's speakeasy brigade, this 'legitimate importer of bracing tonics and fortifying liquid' attracts a cashed-up, fashionable clientele. Inside, it's an atmospheric, brick-vaulted space with excellent cocktails. Prepare to queue later, as it's one of the few late-opening bars of this type. Get there before office-out at 5pm if you want a table. (☎02-9254 8088; www.merivale.com.au/palmer andco; Abercrombie Lane; ⏱5pm-3am Sun-Wed, 3pm-3am Thu & Fri, 4pm-3am Sat; 🛜; 🚆Wynyard)

Grandma's
COCKTAIL BAR

31 ⊗ MAP P62, B4

Billing itself as a 'retrosexual haven of cosmopolitan kitsch and faded granny glamour', Grandma's hits the mark. A stag's head greets you on the stairs and ushers you into a tiny subterranean world of parrot wallpaper and tiki cocktails. Very quirky, very relaxed and casual for a CBD venue. Toasted sandwiches provide sustenance. Look for it behind the Fender shop. (☏02-9264 3004; www.grandmasbarsydney.com.au; Basement, 275 Clarence St; ⊙3pm-midnight Mon-Fri, 5pm-1am Sat; ℞Town Hall)

Establishment
BAR

32 ⊗ MAP P62, C1

Establishment's cashed-up crush proves that the art of swilling cocktails after a hard city day is not lost. Sit at the majestic marble bar or in the swish courtyard, or be absorbed by a leather lounge as stockbrokers scribble their digits on coasters for flirty new acquaintances. The bar was a scene-setter when it opened and is still iconic. (☏02-9240 3100; www.merivale.com/establishmentbar; 252 George St; ⊙11am-late Mon-Fri, noon-late Sat, noon-10pm Sun; ☎; ℞Wynyard)

O Bar
COCKTAIL BAR

33 ⊗ MAP P62, C1

The cocktails at this 47th-floor revolving bar aren't cheap, but they're still substantially cheaper than admission to Sydney Tower (p64) – and it's considerably more glamorous. The views are truly wonderful; get up there shortly after opening time, and kick back to enjoy the sunset and transition into night. There's also smart food on offer. (☏02-9247 9777; www.obardining.com.au; Level 47, Australia Square, 264 George St; ⊙5pm-midnight Sat-Thu, noon-midnight Fri; ☎; ℞Wynyard)

Entertainment

City Recital Hall
CLASSICAL MUSIC

34 ✪ MAP P62, C2

Based on the classic configuration of the 19th-century European concert hall, this custom-built 1200-seat venue boasts near-perfect acoustics. Catch top-flight companies here, such as **Musica Viva** (☏1800 688 482; https://musicaviva.com.au), the **Australian Brandenburg Orchestra** (ABO; ☏02-9328 7581; www.brandenburg.com.au; tickets $70-170) and the **Australian Chamber Orchestra** (ACO; ☏02-8274 3888; www.aco.com.au). (☏02-8256 2222; www.cityrecitalhall.com; 2 Angel Pl; ⊙box office 9am-5pm Mon-Fri; ℞Wynyard)

Metro Theatre
LIVE MUSIC

35 ✪ MAP P62, C6

The Metro is easily Sydney's best mid-sized venue for catching local and alternative international acts in intimate, well-ventilated, easy-seeing comfort. Other offerings include comedy, cabaret and dance parties. (☏02-9550 3666; www.metrotheatre.com.au; 624 George St; ℞Town Hall)

State Theatre
THEATRE

36 ⭐ MAP P62, C4

The 2000-seat State Theatre is a lavish, gilt-ridden, chandelier-dangling palace. It hosts the **Sydney Film Festival** (www.sff.org.au; 🕐Jun), concerts, comedy, opera, musicals and the odd celebrity chef. (📞box office 13 61 00; www.statetheatre.com.au; 49 Market St; 🚉Town Hall)

Shopping

Abbey's
BOOKS

37 🔒 MAP P62, C4

Easily central Sydney's best bookshop, Abbey's has many strengths. It's good on social sciences and has excellent resources for language learning, including a great selection of foreign films on DVD. There's also a big sci-fi and fantasy section. Staff are great and generally very experienced. (📞02-9264 3111; www.abbeys.com.au; 131 York St; 🕐8.30am-6pm Mon-Wed & Fri, to 8pm Thu, 9am-5pm Sat, 10am-5pm Sun; 🚉Town Hall)

Strand Arcade
SHOPPING CENTRE

38 🔒 MAP P62, C3

Constructed in 1891, the beautiful Strand rivals the QVB in the ornateness stakes. The three floors of designer fashions, Australiana and old-world coffee shops will make your shortcut through here considerably longer. Some of the top Australian designers and other iconic brands have stores here – chocolatiers included! Aesop, Haighs, Leona Edmiston, Dinosaur Designs and more are all present. (📞02-9265 6800; www.strandarcade.com.au; 412 George St; 🕐9am-5.30pm Mon-Wed & Fri, to 9pm Thu, to 4pm Sat, 11am-4pm Sun; 🚉Town Hall)

Queen Victoria Building
SHOPPING CENTRE

The QVB (see 1 🔵 Map p62, C4) takes up a whole block and boasts nearly 200 shops on five levels. It's a neo-Gothic masterpiece – without doubt Sydney's most beautiful shopping centre. (QVB; 📞02-9265 6800; www.qvb.com.au; 455 George St; 🕐9am-6pm Mon-Wed, Fri & Sat, to 9pm Thu, 11am-5pm Sun; 🚉Town Hall)

Strand Arcade

STRUCTURESXX/SHUTTERSTOCK ©

Red Eye Records

MUSIC

39 🔒 MAP P62, C4

Partners of music freaks beware: don't let them descend the stairs into this shop unless you are prepared for a lengthy delay. The shelves are stocked with an irresistible collection of new, classic, rare and collectable LPs, CDs, rock T-shirts, books, posters and music DVDs. (📞02-9267 7440; www.redeye. com.au; 143 York St; 🕑9am-6pm Mon-Wed, Fri & Sat, to 9pm Thu, 10am-5pm Sun; 🚇Town Hall)

Paspaley

JEWELLERY

40 🔒 MAP P62, C2

This shell-shaped shop sells lustrous pearls farmed along uninhabited coastline, from Darwin in the Northern Territory to Dampier in Western Australia. Classic and modern designs start at $450 for a ring, rising to more than $1 million for a hefty strand of perfect pink pearls. (📞02-9232 7633; www. paspaley.com; 2 Martin Pl; 🕑10am-6pm Mon-Wed & Fri, to 7.30pm Thu, to 5pm Sat, 11am-5pm Sun; 🚇Martin Place)

Strand Hatters

FASHION & ACCESSORIES

Got a cold or wet head, or a serious case of the *Crocodile Dundees*? Strand Hatters (see 38 🔒 Map p62, C3) will cover your crown with a classically Australian Akubra bush hat (made from rabbit felt). Staff will block and steam hats to customer requirements (crocodile-teeth hatbands cost extra). (📞02-9231 6884; www.strandhatters.com.au; Strand Arcade, 412 George St; 🕑9am-5.30pm Mon-Wed & Fri, to 8pm Thu, to 4pm Sat, 11am-4pm Sun,; 🚇Queen Victoria Building, 🚇Town Hall)

Paddy's Markets

MARKET

41 🔒 MAP P62, B7

Cavernous, thousand-stall Paddy's is the Sydney equivalent of Istanbul's Grand Bazaar, but swap the hookahs and carpets for mobilephone covers, Eminem T-shirts and cheap sneakers. Pick up a VB singlet or wander the aisles in capitalist awe. (www.paddysmarkets. com.au; 9-13 Hay St; 🕑10am-6pm Wed-Sun; 🚇Paddy's Markets, 🚇Central)

Karlangu

ARTS & CRAFTS

42 🔒 MAP P62, B2

Some excellent Aboriginal art is for sale at this gallery near Wynyard, and staff are knowledgable and helpful. They can also arrange packing and postage. (📞02-9279 2700; www.karlangu.com; 47 York St; 🕑9.30am-6pm Mon-Fri, 10am-6pm Sat & Sun; 🚇Wynyard)

Explore ✦
Darling Harbour & Pyrmont

Unashamedly tourist-focused, Darling Harbour will do its best to tempt you to its shoreline bars and restaurants with fireworks displays and a sprinkling of glitz. On its western flank, Pyrmont, though it appears to be sinking under the weight of its casino and motorway flyovers, still has a historic feel in parts, and strolling its harbourside wharves is a real pleasure.

Every other inch of this former dockland is given over to visitor amusements, bars and restaurants. It makes sense to start at Wynyard station and head for Barangaroo South (p81) through the tunnel. From here, following the curve of the bay right around to the other side will take you past most of the key sights, as well as numerous waterfront restaurants and bars. Next, dive into Pyrmont for historic converted warehouses and a more local Sydney scene. If you like, there's some sensational harbourside strolling here, far removed from the tourist beat.

Getting There & Around

🚃 The eastern edge of Darling Harbour is within walking distance of Town Hall train station. For King Street Wharf and Barangaroo South, Wynyard station is closer.

🚋 There are light-rail stops all through Pyrmont.

⛴ Ferry wharves at Barangaroo and Pyrmont Bay.

Darling Harbour & Pyrmont Map on p78

Wharves at Darling Harbour JOONHWAN LEE/SHUTTERSTOCK ©

Sydney Harbour
(Port Jackson)

BARANGAROO

0 ____ 200 m
0 ____ 0.1 miles

1

Pyrmont
Point Park

Jones
Bay
Wharf

Darling
Point

17

12

Hickson Rd

Barangaroo

15

7 Barangaroo
South

10

2

Point St

Herbert St

Pirrama Rd

Darling Island Rd

Bowman St

Community
Park

13

Pyrmont
Bay

18

Darling
Harbour

Lime St

Shelley St

Erskine St

Western Distributor

3

John St

Jones Bay Rd

The Star

*The
Star*

24

9

16

Pirrama St

Edward St

Pyrmont
Bay Park

**Pyrmont
Bay**

Pyrmont
Bay

Australian
National
Maritime
Museum

Darling
Harbour

11

Wild Life
Sydney Zoo

Sydney
Sea Life
Aquarium

5 6

4

Madame
Tussauds

Harris St

Mount St

Pyrmont St

PYRMONT

14

Paternoster Rd

**Pyrmont
Bay**

20

Union St

1

4

Miller St

Little Mount St

Harris St

Bulwara Rd

**Fish
Market**

19

Bunn St

Murray St

Harbourside

Cockle
Bay

Pyrmont Bridge

5

Bank St

*Sydney
Fish
Market*

2

Experiment St

Ada Pl

Harris St

**Convention
Centre**

Allen St

Pyrmont St

Darling Dr

21

Pyrmont Bridge Rd

Wattle Cres

Wentworth
Park

Wentworth
Park

Western Distributor

23

Fig St

Harris St

**DARLING
HARBOUR**

Tumbalong
Park

8

6

Ada Pl

**Exhibition
Centre**

*Chinese Garden
of Friendship*

22

3

For reviews see	
⊙ Sights	p79
⊗ Eating	p82
⊙ Drinking	p84
☆ Entertainment	p85

Sights

Australian National Maritime Museum
MUSEUM

1 ◎ MAP P78, C4

Beneath a soaring roof, the Maritime Museum sails through Australia's inextricable relationship with the sea. Exhibitions range from Indigenous canoes to surf culture, immigration to the navy. The worthwhile 'big ticket' (adult/child $32/20) includes entry to some of the vessels moored outside, including the atmospheric submarine HMAS *Onslow* and the destroyer HMAS *Vampire*. The high-production-value short film *Action Stations* sets the mood with a re-creation of a mission event from each vessel. Excellent free **guided tours** explain each vessel's features.

You can also visit a lighthouse and an 1874 square rigger, the *James Craig,* which periodically offers **sailing trips** (📞02-9298 3888; www.shf.org.au; Wharf 7, Pyrmont; adult/child from $120/60; 🚢Pyrmont Bay, 🚊The Star). Normally a replica of Cook's *Endeavour* also drops anchor here. There's plenty to do for kids, especially at weekends. Other parts of the museum include a free exhibition on wooden boats in the next building north, and, opposite Pyrmont Bay ferry stop, the **Welcome Wall**, a commemoration of migration to Australia that seems particularly relevant in the current political climate. (📞02-9298 3777; www.anmm.gov.au; 2 Murray St, Pyrmont; permanent collection free, temporary exhibitions adult/child $20/free; ⏰9.30am-5pm, to 6pm Jan; 🚻; 🚌389, 🚢Pyrmont Bay)

Sydney Fish Market
MARKET

2 ◎ MAP P78, A5

This piscatorial precinct on Blackwattle Bay shifts over 15 million kilograms of seafood annually, and has retail outlets, restaurants, a sushi bar, an oyster bar, and a highly regarded **cooking school** (📞02-9004 1111; www.sydneyfishmarket.com.au/seafood-school; Sydney Fish Market, Pyrmont Bridge Rd, Pyrmont; 2-/4-hr courses $90/165). Chefs, locals and overfed seagulls haggle over mud crabs, Balmain bugs, lobsters and slabs of salmon at the daily fish auction, which kicks off at 5.30am weekdays. Check it out on a behind-the-scenes tour (adult/child $35/10). (📞02-9004 1108; www.sydneyfishmarket.com.au; Bank St, Pyrmont; ⏰7am-4pm Mon-Thu, to 5pm Fri-Sun; 🚊Fish Market)

Chinese Garden of Friendship
GARDENS

3 ◎ MAP P78, D6

Built according to Taoist principles, the Chinese Garden of Friendship is usually an oasis of tranquillity – although one increasingly dwarfed by assertive modern buildings. Designed by architects from Guangzhou (Sydney's sister city) for Australia's bicentenary in 1988, the garden interweaves pavilions, waterfalls, lakes, paths and lush plant life. There's also a **tea house**. (📞02-9240 8888; www.chinesegarden.com.au; Harbour St, Central Sydney; adult/child $6/3; ⏰9.30am-5pm Apr-Sep, to 5.30pm Oct-Mar; 🚇Town Hall)

Sydney Sea Life Aquarium

AQUARIUM

4 ◎ MAP P78, D4

As well as regular wall-mounted tanks and ground-level enclosures, this impressive complex has two large pools that you can walk through – safely enclosed in Perspex tunnels – as an intimidating array of sharks and rays pass overhead. Other highlights include clownfish (g'day, Nemo!), platypuses, moon jellyfish (in a disco-lit tube), sea dragons and the swoon-worthy finale: the two-million-litre Great Barrier Reef tank.

The aquarium's two dugongs were rescued after washing up orphaned on Queensland beaches. Attempts to return them to the wild failed, so the Dugong Island enclosure was built to house them. As sad as it is to see such large marine mammals in captivity, it offers a fascinating and rare opportunity to get close to them. Needless to say, kids

---

Sydney's Chinese Community

Chinese immigrants started to come to Australia around 1840, when convict transportation ceased and labouring jobs became freely available. Initially they were considered a solution to labour shortages, but as gold-rush fever took hold, racial intolerance grew. The tireless Chinese were seen as threats, and state entry restrictions were enforced from the early 19th century into much of the 20th century.

In 1861 the NSW government enacted the White Australia policy, aimed at reducing the influx of Chinese. This included a ban on naturalisation, work-permit restrictions and acts such as the 1861 *Chinese Immigration Regulation & Restriction Act* (an immigrant tax). As a result of this policy (and the fact that many Chinese people returned to China after the gold rush), the Chinese population remained low. The White Australia policy wasn't completely dismantled until 1973.

Sydney's Chinese community eventually gravitated to Dixon St near Darling Harbour, an area once known for opium and gambling but now better known for tasty and great-value food.

A major immigration wave from pre-handover Hong Kong boosted the Cantonese population in the 1980s and 1990s; more recently there has been a strong increase in arrivals from the mainland, as well as a very significant temporary population of students.

Today people of Chinese extraction make up some 10% of Sydney's population, with around half of these born in Australia.

love this place; arrive early to beat the crowds. It's cheaper to book online, and there are various combo deals with other attractions run by the same company, including the zoo and Madame Tussauds. (📞02-8251 7800; www.sydneyaquarium.com.au; Aquarium Pier, Central Sydney; adult/child $42/30; ⏲9.30am-6pm; 🚆Town Hall)

Wild Life Sydney Zoo   ZOO

5 ◎ MAP P78, D4

Complementing its sister and neighbour, Sea Life, this large complex houses an impressive collection of Australian native reptiles, butterflies, spiders, snakes and mammals (including kangaroos and koalas). The nocturnal section is particularly good, bringing out the extrovert in the quolls, potoroos, echidnas and possums. As interesting as Wild Life is, it's not a patch on Taronga Zoo (p51). Still, it's worth considering as part of a combo with Sea Life, or if you're short on time. Tickets are cheaper online. (📞02-9333 9245; www.wildlifesydney.com.au; Aquarium Pier, Central Sydney; adult/child $42/30; ⏲9.30am-5pm; 🚆Town Hall)

Madame Tussauds   MUSEUM

6 ◎ MAP P78, D4

In this celebrity-obsessed age, it's hardly surprising that Madame Tussauds' hyperrealistic waxwork dummies are just as popular now as when the eponymous madame lugged her macabre haul of French Revolution death masks to London in 1803. Where else do mere mortals get to strike a pose with Hugh Jackman and cosy up to Kylie? There are various combination entrance deals with the adjacent zoo and aquarium; book online for best rates. (www.madametussauds.com.au; Aquarium Pier, Central Sydney; adult/child $42/30; ⏲9.30am-6pm; 🚆Town Hall)

Barangaroo South   AREA

7 ◎ MAP P78, D2

The latest product of Sydney's port redevelopment is this extension of the CBD's office-land. There are three rather lofty skyscrapers and pedestrian alleys beneath, busy with corporate types rushing about, coffee in hand. On the harbourfront itself is a handsome promenade with lots of decent bars and eateries, merging into the similar King Street Wharf and Cockle Bay strips to the south. The food is generally better at Barangaroo than the other two. There's a major ferry stop here, too. (www.thestreetsofbarangaroo.com; Central Sydney; 🚢Barangaroo, 🚆Wynyard)

Tumbalong Park   PARK

8 ◎ MAP P78, D6

Flanked by the modern **Darling Walk** development, this grassy circle on Darling Harbour's southern rump is set up for family fun. Sunbakers and frisbee-throwers occupy the lawns, tourists dunk their feet in fountains on hot summer afternoons and there's an excellent children's playground with a 21m flying fox (zip line). (Harbour St, Central Sydney; ![icon]; ![icon] Town Hall)

Eating

Café Court
FOOD HALL $

 9 ![icon] MAP P78, B3

The Star has done a great job of filling its ground-floor food court with some of the best operators of their kind, with top-quality dumpling rollers, fish 'n' chip fryers, patisserie wizards and gelato makers. (www.star.com.au; The Star, 80 Pyrmont St, Pyrmont; ⏰11am-9pm Sun & Mon, to 11pm Tue-Sat; ![icon]; ![icon] The Star)

Anason
TURKISH $$

10 ![icon] MAP P78, D2

Outdoor eating is a pleasure of the new Barangaroo strip, and this is one of the best places to do it. Modern takes on generous Turkish flavours are upbeat and delicious, with plenty of breads and dippable dishes alongside grilled seafood and hearty meat. It gets very busy in the noon-to-2pm lunch break. (![icon]02-9188 1581; www.anason.com.au; 5/23 Barangaroo Ave, Central Sydney; mains $24-36; ⏰11.30am-11pm; ![icon]Barangaroo, ![icon]Wynyard)

Malaya
MALAYSIAN $$

11 ![icon] MAP P78, D3

There's something really life-affirming about quality Malaysian cooking, and what you get here is certainly that. Dishes bursting with flavour and spice make it a very authentic experience, while fabulous views over Darling Harbour (fireworks on Saturday nights) add romance. The atmosphere is a very Sydney blend of upmarket and casual. À la carte is better than the set menu. (![icon]02-9279 1170; www.themalaya.com.au; 39 Lime St, Central Sydney; mains $26-35; ⏰noon-3pm & 6-10pm Mon-Fri, noon-3pm & 5.30-10pm Sat, 5.30-10pm Sun; ![icon]![icon]; ![icon]Barangaroo, ![icon]Wynyard)

Cafe Morso
CAFE $$

12 ![icon] MAP P78, A1

On pretty Jones Bay Wharf, this makes a fine venue for breakfast or lunch (though it gets busy, so you may want to book). There's a mixture of Channel 7 workers and yacht skippers. Sassy breakfasts – try the bacon gnocchi – morph into proper cooked lunches, or you can just grab a sandwich. (![icon]02-9692 0111; www.cafemorso.com.au; Jones Bay Wharf, Pyrmont; breakfast $13-20, lunch mains $18-28; ⏰7am-3.30pm Mon-Fri, 9am-2.30pm Sat, 8am-3.30pm Sun; ![icon]![icon]; ![icon]The Star)

LuMi
ITALIAN $$$

13 ![icon] MAP P78, B2

This wharf spot sits right alongside the bobbing boats, though views aren't quite knock-me-down. Hidden just steps from the Star, it offers casual competence and strikingly innovative Italian-Japanese fusion cuisine. The degustation is a tour de force;

memorable creations include extraordinary pasta dishes. The open kitchen is always entertaining, service is smart and both wine and sake lists are great. (📞02-9571 1999; www.lumidining. com; 56 Pirrama Rd, Pyrmont; 7/10 courses $120/150, 5-course lunch Fri $85; ⏰6.30-10.30pm Wed & Thu, noon-2.30pm & 6-10.30pm Fri-Sun; 📶; 🚇Pyrmont Bay, 🚃The Star)

Sokyo

JAPANESE $$$

14 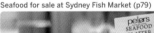 MAP P78, B4

Bringing an injection of Toyko glam to the edge of the casino complex, Sokyo serves well-crafted sushi and sashimi, delicate tempura, tasty robata grills and sophisticated mains. It also dishes up Sydney's best Japanese-style breakfast. Solo travellers should grab a counter seat by the sushi kitchen to watch all the action unfurl. (📞02-9657 9161; www.star.com.au/sokyo; The Star, 80 Pyrmont St, Pyrmont; breakfast $23-38, mains $32-65; ⏰7-10.30am & 5.30-10pm Sun-Thu, 7-10.30am, noon-2pm & 5.30-10.30pm Fri & Sat; 📶🍴; 🚃The Star)

Cirrus

SEAFOOD $$$

15 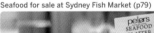 MAP P78, D1

The curved glass windows of this excellent new Barangaroo seafood restaurant offer a water view more ambient than spectacular, but the tinny (simple fishing boat) suspended from the ceiling hints at another focus. Sustainably sourced fish and extremely tasty molluscs and crustaceans form the backbone of the menu, which

Seafood for sale at Sydney Fish Market (p79)

features dishes with exquisite flavour pairings and presentation, designed to share.

The wine list is first-class, with lots of imports and carafe options. (☎02-9220 0111; www.cirrusdining.com.au; 10/23 Barangaroo Ave, Central Sydney; mains $38-56; ☺noon-3pm & 6-10.30pm; ☻Barangaroo, ☒Wynyard)

Momofuku Seiōbo
MODERN AUSTRALIAN $$$

16 ⊗ MAP P78, B3

The first restaurant outside the US opened by New York's gastronomic darling David Chang, Momofuku Seiōbo is a key foodie favourite. Bringing together the techniques, concepts and ideas of Japanese *kaiseki* (multi-course eating) and classical Western degustation, it's not one for the short of time, or funds. (☎02-9657 9169; www.seiobo.momofuku.com; The Star, 80 Pyrmont Street, Pyrmont; degustation menu $185; ☺6-10pm Mon-Fri, noon-2pm & 6-10pm Sat; ☒The Star)

Flying Fish
SEAFOOD $$$

17 ⊗ MAP P78, B1

On a lovely Pyrmont wharf, this is everything a seafood restaurant should be, with crisp white tablecloths, gleaming glasses and water views. Romance and city lights work their magic here, aided by excellent food and an indulgent cocktail list. Its toilets are the coolest in town – the clear glass frosts over when you close the stall door.

The little **cocktail bar** is a pleasant destination in itself, a fine place to lounge harbourside away from the bustle. (☎02-9518 6677; www.flyingfish.com.au; Jones Bay Wharf, Pyrmont; mains $40-50; ☺6-10.30pm Mon, noon-2.30pm & 6-10.30pm Tue-Sat, noon-2.30pm Sun; ☒The Star)

Bea
MODERN AUSTRALIAN $$$

18 ⊗ MAP P78, D2

Looking like a double-decker salad burger with its concentric rings and verdant planter boxes, **Barangaroo House** is a striking addition to Sydney's waterfront. Halfway up, this upbeat bistro offers super outdoor seating and tighter indoor tables. Fusion ingredients are spiced up with bush tucker; the *umami* kick of tyrant ants on asparagus is a standout. Some great wines populate a fat list. (Barangaroo House; ☎02-8587 5400; www.barangaroohouse.com.au; 35 Barangaroo Ave, Central Sydney; mains $32-48; ☺noon-3pm & 5.30-11pm; ☎; ☻Barangaroo, ☒Wynyard)

Drinking

Smoke
COCKTAIL BAR

On the top floor of the new Barangaroo House building, Smoke (see 18 ⊗ Map p78, D2) has a most pleasant outlook over the busy comings and goings at the ferry wharf below. It takes cocktails seriously – the seasonal G&T is a standout dose of refreshment. Get here early to bag one of the outdoor tables before the 5pm office crowd invades. (☎02-8587 5400; www.barangaroohouse.com.au; 35 Barangaroo Ave, Central Sydney; ☺3pm-midnight Mon-Wed, noon-midnight Thu-Sun; ☎; ☻Barangaroo, ☒Wynyard)

Peg Leg
BAR

19 MAP P78, B4

In what was once one of Sydney's older hotels, this small bar has a pirate theme and a feel of the Spanish Main. It's got plenty of interesting spirits, including quality rum. It takes food seriously and the little wood-clad dining area is a great place for seafood and steak grills. (www.facebook.com/pegleg pyrmont; 11 Pyrmont Bridge Rd, Pyrmont; ☺3pm-midnight Mon-Thu, 11am-midnight Fri-Sun; ☒Pyrmont Bay)

Pyrmont Bridge Hotel
PUB

20 MAP P78, B4

Standing like a guardian of tradition at the entrance to Pyrmont, this solid pub is a bastion of no-frills Sydney drinking culture. With an island bar and rooftop terrace, there are many handsome features; there's also lots of character and regular live music. Its biggest selling point is its 24-hour license – the CBD lockout zone ends several metres away. In practice, it usually closes for an hour or two around 5am.(☎02-9660 6996; www.pyrmontbridgehotel.com; 96 Union St, Pyrmont; ☺24hr; ☋; ☒Pyrmont Bay)

Home
BAR, CLUB

21 MAP P78, D5

Welcome to the pleasuredome: a three-level, 2100-capacity timber-and-glass 'prow' that's home to a dance floor, countless bars, outdoor balconies, and sonics that make other clubs sound like transistor radios. The club often features big-name DJs; you can catch live music most nights at the attached **Tokio Hotel bar** downstairs (www.tokiohotellive.com.au). (☎02-9266 0600; www.homesydney.com; 1 Wheat Rd, Cockle Bay Wharf, Central Sydney; ☺club 9pm-4am Thu-Sat, 10pm-4am Sun; ☋; ☒Town Hall)

Entertainment

ICC Sydney
LIVE MUSIC, THEATRE

22 MAP P78, C6

The shiny new International Convention Centre at Darling Harbour has three theatres, including one that seats 8000, and principally holds big touring bands. It replaces the former Entertainment Centre. (☎02-8297 7600; www.iccsydney.com.au; Darling Dr; ☒Exhibition Centre)

Monkey Baa Theatre Company
THEATRE

23 MAP P78, D5

Bring your budding culture vultures here to watch Australian children's books come to life. This energetic company devises and stages its own adaptations. (☎02-8624 9340; www.monkeybaa.com.au; 1 Harbour St, Central Sydney; tickets around $25; ☖; ☒Town Hall)

Sydney Lyric Theatre
THEATRE

24 MAP P78, B3

This high-quality 2000-seat theatre within the Star casino stages big-name musicals and the occasional concert. (☎02-9509 3600; www.sydneylyric.com.au; The Star, Pirrama Rd, Pyrmont; ☒The Star)

Explore ◈

Inner West

The bohemian sweep of the Inner West is an array of suburbs crowded with great places to eat and drink. The quiet streets of Glebe and louder Newtown, grouped around the University of Sydney, are the most well-known of these tightly packed suburbs, but Enmore, Marrickville, Summer Hill, Petersham and more are all worth investigating. All the essential hangouts for students – bookshops, cafes and pubs – are present in abundance, but the Inner West is a lifestyle choice for a whole swathe of Sydney society.

The Inner West is a sociological stew of students, urban hippies, lifestyle-focused professional couples, artists and more. The most high-profile suburb, Newtown, where stoners and home renovators collide, shadows sinuous King St, lined with quirky boutiques, bookshops, yoga studios, cafes and Thai restaurants. It's climbing the social rungs, but is still free-thinking and bolshy.

Getting There & Around

🚆 Central and Redfern train stations are handy for Darlington and Chippendale, while Newtown and several other suburbs have their own station.

🚊 Glebe has two light-rail stops.

🚌 Buses from the city ply Glebe Point Rd (370, 431–433), Parramatta Rd (413, 436–440, 461, 480–483, M10) and City Rd/King St (352, 370, 422–428, M30).

Inner West Map on p90

Powerhouse Museum (p92) SARAHI810/SHUTTERSTOCK ©

Walking Tour 🥾

Studying the University of Sydney

Australia's oldest tertiary institution (1850) has well over 50,000 students and even boasts its own postcode. You don't need to have a PhD to grab a free campus map and wander around. The university completely dominates the surrounding suburbs of Camperdown, Darlington, Chippendale, and to a lesser extent, Glebe and Newtown.

Walk Facts

Start Verge Gallery
Finish Sappho Books
Length 1.8km, 45 minutes

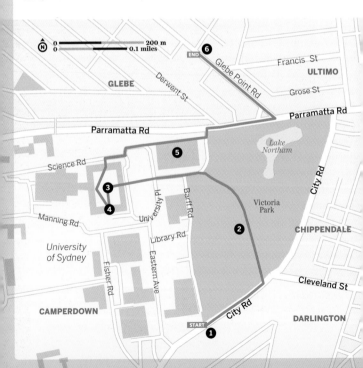

❶ Head to the Verge

On the Darlington side of City Road, this university-affiliated **gallery** (📞02-9563 6218; www. verge-gallery.net; City Rd, Darlington; admission free; 🕙10am-5pm Tue-Fri, 11am-4pm Sat; 🚌352, 370, 422, 423, 426, 428, M30, 🚆Redfern) has two exhibition spaces and a mission to get people involved with the artworks via a program of talks and other activities.

❷ Venture into Victoria Park

The green gateway to the Inner West and the University of Sydney, **Victoria Park** (cnr Parramatta & City Rds; 🚌352, 370, 422, 423, 426, 428, M30) is a 9-hectare grassy wedge revolving around pond-like Lake Northam. The 50m pool here serves as Newtown and Glebe's beach.

❸ Cross the Quadrangle

Flanked by two grand halls that wouldn't be out of place in Harry Potter's beloved Hogwarts, the Quadrangle has a Gothic Revival design that tips its mortarboard towards the stately colleges of Oxford. It was designed by colonial architect Edmund Blacket and completed in 1862; he also built St Andrew's Cathedral in the city.

❹ Nick into the Nicholson

The **Nicholson Museum** (📞02-9351 2812; www.sydney.edu.au/museums; University Pl, University of Sydney; admission free; 🕙10am-4.30pm Mon-Fri, noon-4pm 1st Sat of month; 🚌412, 413, 436, 438-40, 461, 480, 483, M10) is a must see for ancient history geeks, with a beautifully displayed collection of Greek, Roman, Cypriot, Egyptian and Near Eastern antiquities and a marvellous Lego Pompeii. In 2020 the Nicholson will be incorporated into the new Chau Chak Wing Museum.

❺ Check out the Chau Chak Wing

Billionaire Chinese Australian property developer Chau Chak Wing made a substantial donation towards the cost of this new **museum** (📞02-9351 2222; http://sydney.edu.au; University Pl, University of Sydney; admission free; 🚌412, 413, 436, 438-40, 461, 480, 483, M10), which is to open in 2020. As well as incorporating the Nicholson Museum, it will also display the university's art, natural history and ethnographic collections.

❻ Slink into Sappho Books

Combining the essentials of student life – books, coffee, alcohol and lesbian poetry – Sappho has a beaut bohemian garden **cafe** (📞02-9552 4498; www.sapphobooks. com.au; 51 Glebe Point Rd, Glebe; light meals $6-19; 🕙8.30am-6pm Mon-Sat, 9am-6pm Sun; 📶; 🚌431, 433, 🚏Glebe), its walls scrawled with generations of graffiti. Wine and tapas kick in after 6pm.

Inner West

PYRMONT

Harris St

Pier St

Powerhouse Museum

Exhibition Centre

Bulwarra Rd

Jones St

William Henry St

Quarry Rd

Bulwarra Rd

Mary Ann St

ULTIMO

Thomas St

UTS

Central

Broadway

Abercrombie St

Knox St

CHIPPENDALE

City Rd

White Rabbit

Wattle St

Mountain St

Bay St

Greek St

Francis St

Lake Northam

Victoria Park

Science Rd

Wentworth Park

Wentworth Park

Bridge Rd

Bellevue St

Darghan St

Darling St

Broughton St

Glebe St

Glebe Point Rd

St Johns Rd

Mt Vernon St

Westmoreland St

Catherine St

Parramatta Rd

Blackwattle Bay

Blackwattle Park

Glebe

Gottenham St

Talfourd St

Derwent St

Reuss St

GLEBE

Ferry Rd

Forsyth St

Avona Ave

Cook St

Stewart St

Glebe Point Rd

St James Reserve

Hereford St

St Phillip St

Bridge Rd

Forest Rd

Ross St

FOREST LODGE

Allen St

Mansfield St

Boyce St

Wigram Rd

Toxteth Rd

Arcadia Rd

Edward St

Avenue Rd

Jubilee Park

Charles St

Ross St

Minogue Cres

Lewis Hoad Reserve

Bridge Rd

Barr St

Booth St

Pyrmont Bridge Rd

Parramatta Rd

Manning Rd

Bicentennial Park

Federal Park

Jubilee Park

Johnstons Creek

The Crescent

ANNANDALE

Trafalgar St

Nelson St

Booth St

Taylor St

Nelson St

Hogan Park

Johnston St

500 m
0.25 miles

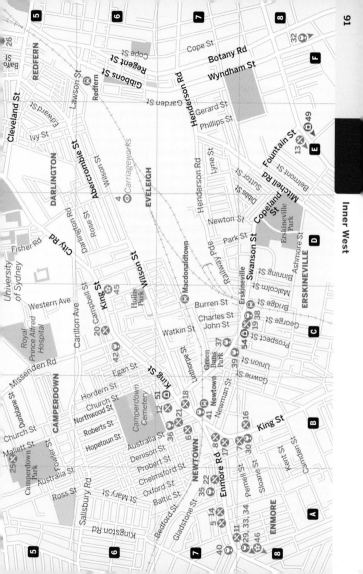

Sights

White Rabbit — GALLERY

1 ◉ MAP P90, F4

If you're an art lover or a bit of a Mad Hatter, this particular rabbit hole will leave you grinning like a Cheshire Cat. There are so many works in this private collection of cutting-edge, contemporary Chinese art that only a fraction can be displayed at one time. Who knew that the People's Republic was turning out work that was so edgy, funny, sexy and idiosyncratic? It's probably Sydney's best contemporary art gallery. There's an on-site tearoom. (📞02-8399 2867; www.whiterabbitcollection.org; 30 Balfour St, Chippendale; admission free; 🕙10am-5pm Wed-Sun, closed Feb & Aug; 🚉Central)

Powerhouse Museum — MUSEUM

2 ◉ MAP P90, F2

A short walk from Darling Harbour, this cavernous science and design museum whirs away inside the former power station for Sydney's defunct, original tram network. The collection and temporary exhibitions cover everything from robots and life on Mars to steam trains to climate change to atoms to fashion, industrial design and avant-garde art installations. There are great options for kids of all ages but it's equally intriguing for adults. Grab a map of the museum once you're inside. Disabled access is good.

The Powerhouse is due to move to a new location in Parramatta that is set to be completed in 2022. (Museum of Applied Arts & Sciences/MAAS; 📞02-9217 0111; www.powerhousemuseum.com; 500 Harris St, Ultimo; adult/child $15/free; 🕙10am-5pm; ♿; 🚉Exhibition Centre)

Central Park — AREA

3 ◉ MAP P90, F4

Occupying the site of an old brewery, this major residential and shopping development is a striking sight. Most impressive is Jean Nouvel's award-winning, vertical-garden-covered tower, **One Central Park**. The cantilevered platform high above has been designed to reflect sunlight onto the greenery below. Its lower floors have plenty of food options, **cinemas** (📞02-9190 2290; www.palacecinemas.com.au; Level 3, Central Park, 28 Broadway, Chippendale; 🚉Central), shops, a supermarket and gallery spaces, while adjacent Kensington St and Spice Alley (p95) offer further gastronomic pleasure. Two new Norman Foster–designed apartment towers, **Duo**, are under construction. (📞02-8096 9900; www.centralparksydney.com; 28 Broadway, Chippendale; 🕙10am-8pm; 🚉Central)

Carriageworks — ARTS CENTRE

4 ◉ MAP P90, D6

Built between 1880 and 1889, this intriguing group of huge Victorian-era workshops was part of the

Eveleigh Railyards. The rail workers chugged out in 1988, and in 2007 the artists moved in. It's now home to various avant-garde arts and performance projects, and there's usually something interesting to check out; have a look on the website to see what's on. There's a very pleasant cafe-bar here and an excellent Saturday morning farmers market (p105). (☎02-8571 9099; www.carriageworks.com.au; 245 Wilson St, Eveleigh; admission free; ◷10am-6pm; ☒Redfern)

Eating

Cow & the Moon   ICE CREAM $

5 ☒ MAP P90, A7

Forget the diet and slink into this cool corner cafe, where an array of sinful truffles and tasty tarts

beckons seductively. Ignore them and head straight for the world's best gelato – the title this humble little place won in 2014 at the Gelato World Tour title in Rimini, Italy. There's decent coffee too. (☎02-9557 4255; 181 Enmore Rd, Enmore; small gelati $6.50; ◷8.30am-10.30pm Sun-Thu, to 11.30pm Fri & Sat; ⊚✎♿; ☒Newtown)

Black Star Pastry   BAKERY $

6 ☒ MAP P90, B7

Wise folks follow the black star to pay homage to excellent coffee, a large selection of sweet things and a few very good savoury things (gourmet pies and the like). There are only a couple of tables; it's more a snack-and-run or picnic-in-the-park kind of place. Prepare to queue. Other outposts have cropped up

Cow & the Moon

around town. (📞02-9557 8656; www.
blackstarpastry.com.au; 277 Australia St,
Newtown; snacks $4-10; ⏰7am-5pm
Sun-Wed, 7am-5.30pm Thu-Sat; 🖉;
🚃Newtown)

Lentil as Anything VEGETARIAN $

7 ❌ MAP P90, B8

With tasty vegetarian and vegan
fare on a voluntary contribution
basis, this heartening project
brings people together at communal tables. It's deservedly popular
with everyone, from latte-sipping
laptoppers to backpackers,
students and some people who
really need the feed. For those not
in the know, the name is a pun on
legendary Australian pop-rockers
Mental as Anything. (📞02-8283
5580; www.lentilasanything.com; 391
King St, Newtown; donation; ⏰noon-
3pm & 6-9pm Mon-Fri, 10am-3pm &
6-9pm Sat & Sun; 🖉; 🚃Newtown)

Golden Lotus VEGAN, VIETNAMESE $

8 ❌ MAP P90, B7

Delicious bowls of pho, crunchy
textures and fresh flavour bursts
make this perhaps the best of
Newtown's sizeable crop of vegan
and vegetarian restaurants. As well
as vegetable-based meals, there
are lots of dishes involving soy-
based chicken and fish substitutes.
It's BYO alcohol. (📞02-8937 2838;
www.goldenlotus-vegan.com; 343 King
St, Newtown; mains $14-18; ⏰5.30-
10.30pm Mon-Wed, noon-3pm & 5.30-
10.30pm Thu-Sun; 🖉; 🚃Newtown)

Wedge CAFE $

9 ❌ MAP P90, D3

Cut a corridor out of the side of a
building, open it to the street and
add artful industrial decor and you
have the Wedge, which has delicious single-origin espressos and

Out in the Inner West

Newtown's King St and Enmore Rd are among the city's most diverse
eating streets, with Thai restaurants sitting alongside Vietnamese,
Greek, Lebanese and Mexican, but the scene is replicated on a smaller
scale in nearly every inner west suburb. Many restaurants allow you to
BYO wine. When it comes to coffee culture, all roads point this way, too.

And devotees of the comfortable, atmospheric local pub rejoice!
The Inner West has plenty of pubs in varying degrees of gentrification, ranging from 'not at all' to 'within an inch of its life'. A thirsty
student population sustains a barrage of bars and live-music
venues, the hipster crowd means post-ironic cocktail tomfoolery is
gloriously in vogue, and a sizeable lesbian and gay community also
makes its presence felt. Night owls can take heart that the Inner
West is outside the central city's restricted alcohol zone – meaning
no lockouts. Family-friendly pubs with play areas are common.

cold brews as well as wholesome, artfully presented breakfasts, sandwiches and lunch specials. The quality and atmosphere are great, and sitting at the sill gazing over the street is a pleasure. (☑02-9660 3313; www.thewedgeglebe.com; cnr Cowper St & Glebe Point Rd, Glebe; light meals $8-18; ☼7am-4pm Mon-Sat, 8am-3pm Sun; 🛜🖉; 🚌431, 433, 🚆Glebe)

Spice Alley   ASIAN $

10 🍴 MAP P90, F4

This little laneway off Kensington St by Central Park is a picturesque outdoor eating hub serving street-foody dishes from various Asian cuisines. Grab your noodles, dumplings or pork belly and fight for a stool. Quality is reasonable rather than spectacular, but prices are low and it's fun. It's cashless: pay by card or load up a prepay card from the drinks booth.

The drinks booth is soft-drink only, but you can BYO alcohol; there are two bottleshops nearby. ☑02-9281 0822; www.spice-alley.com.au; Kensington St, Chippendale; dishes $8-16; ☼11am-10pm Sun-Wed, to 10.30pm Thu-Sat; 🖉; 🚆Central)

Faheem Fast Food   PAKISTANI $

11 🍴 MAP P90, A8

This Enmore Rd stalwart offers a totally no-frills dining atmosphere but very tasty and authentic curry and tandoori options served until late. Its Haleem lentil-and-beef curry is memorably tasty, while the brain *nihari* is another standout, and not as challenging as it sounds. (☑02-9550 4850; 194 Enmore Rd, Enmore; dishes $12-14; ☼5pm-midnight Mon-Fri, noon-midnight Sat & Sun; 🖉; 🚌423, 426, 428)

Mary's   BURGERS $

12 🍴 MAP P90, B7

Not put off by the grungy aesthetics, the ear-splitting heavy metal or the fact that the graffiti-daubed building was previously a sexual health clinic and a Masonic Temple? Then head up to the mezzanine of this dimly lit hipster bar for some of the best burgers and fried chicken in town. (www.getfat.com.au; 6 Mary St, Newtown; mains $13-18; ☼4pm-midnight Mon-Thu, noon-midnight Fri & Sat, noon-10pm Sun; 🛜🖉; 🚆Newtown)

Grounds of Alexandria   CAFE $$

13 🍴 MAP P90, E8

A quite extraordinary Alexandria spot, the Grounds goes well beyond converted industrial chic. This former pie factory now sports futuristic coffee technology, tip-top baking and delicious food, but it's the enormous garden setting that has the biggest impact: chickens, a waste-chewing pig and greenery all around. It's a real sight to behold. You won't behold it alone though...prepare to queue.

Also here is the **Potting Shed** (mains $24-37; ☼11.30am-9pm Mon-Thu, to 10pm Fri, 11am-10pm Sat, to 9pm Sun; 🛜🖉), another riot of plants open for evening drinks

Potting Shed at the Grounds of Alexandria (p95)

and food. (📞02-9699 2225; www.
thegrounds.com.au; 2 Huntley St,
Alexandria; dishes $15-26; ⏲7am-4pm
Mon-Fri, 7.30am-4pm Sat & Sun; 🛜♿;
🚌348, 🚇Green Square)

Stanbuli
TURKISH $$

15 ❌ MAP P90, A7

Hidden by the vintage pink-and-
purple facade of a '60s hair salon,
this sophisticated exploration
of traditional Istanbul dishes is
excellent. The handsomely tiled
downstairs bar area is a sociable
spot for a shot of raki and some
delicious share plates, or head
upstairs for more formal dining.
Flavours are intense, with an em-
phasis on Mediterranean seafood
and charcoal-grilled meats. (📞02-
8624 3132; www.stanbuli.com.au; 135
Enmore Rd, Enmore; mains $20-30;

⏲6pm-midnight Wed-Sat, to 10pm
Sun; 🚇Newtown)

Koi Dessert Bar
DESSERTS $$

15 ❌ MAP P90, F4

Having made the nation salivate
on *Master Chef Australia*, Reynold
Poernomo now produces his
fabulous desserts for public con-
sumption at this two-level spot by
Central Park. Downstairs is a cafe
with scrumptious sweet fare on
offer. Pre-book and head upstairs
(6pm to 9.30pm) for the ultimate
luxury; a four-course dessert degustation. It also does a savoury
degustation menu. (📞02-9212
1230; www.koidessertbar.com.au; 46
Kensington St, Chippendale; dessert
degustation $65; ⏲10am-10pm Tue-
Sun; 🚇Central)

Bloodwood   MODERN AUSTRALIAN $$

16 🍴 MAP P90, B8

Relax over a few drinks and a progression of small plates (we love those polenta chips!) in the front bar, or make your way to the rear to enjoy soundly conceived and expertly cooked dishes from across the globe. The decor is industrial-chic and the vibe is alternative – very Newtown. (☏02-9557 7699; www.bloodwoodnewtown.com; 416 King St, Newtown; share plates $17-32; 🕓5-11pm Mon-Fri, noon-3pm & 5-11pm Sat & Sun; 🍴; 🚇Newtown)

3 Olives   GREEK $$

17 🍴 MAP P90, B7

There's something very life-affirming about a good Greek restaurant, and this family-run *taberna* ticks all the boxes. The decor is restrained, with olive-coloured walls, but there's nothing restrained about the portions or aromas: mounds of perfectly textured BBQ octopus, big chunks of melt-in-the-mouth lamb *kleftiko*, warm flatbread, hearty meatballs and more-ish olives. It's an excellent celebration of traditional eating. (☏02-9557 7754; 365 King St, Newtown; mains $24-27, meze dishes $13-16; 🕓5.30pm-midnight Wed-Sun; 🚇Newtown)

Thai Pothong   THAI $$

18 🍴 MAP P90, B7

The menu at this crowd-pleasing restaurant is full of long-time favourites and people still queue for them. The army of staff are efficient and friendly, and the food reliably excellent. Top choice is a window seat to watch the Newtowners pass by. If you pay cash, you get a discount, paid in a local currency only redeemable in the gift shop. (☏02-9550 6277; www.thaipothong.com.au; 294 King St, Newtown; mains $18-31; 🕓noon-3pm daily, plus 6-10.30pm Mon-Thu, 6-11pm Fri & Sat, 5.30-10pm Sun; 🅿🍴; 🚇Newtown)

Maggie's   THAI $$

19 🍴 MAP P90, C8

Worth the short stroll downhill from the Newtown strip, or as the focus of a night out in pleasant Erskineville itself, this small neighbourhood Thai restaurant is a real gem. A short menu and blackboard specials offer intense, flavour-packed dishes from the open kitchen with great presentation and some unusual flavours. Intelligent service adds to the experience, as does outdoor seating. (☏02-9516 5270; www.maggiesthai.com.au; 75 Erskineville Rd, Erskineville; mains $18-26; 🕓5-9pm Sat-Wed, 11am-2.30pm & 5-9pm Thu & Fri; 🍴; 🚇Erskineville)

Thanh Binh   VIETNAMESE $$

20 🍴 MAP P90, C6

This old Vietnamese favourite isn't top of the trend meter any more, but it should be for its wide range of consistently delicious dishes. Favourites are soft-shell crab on papaya salad or sinful pork belly and quail eggs in stock. Other dishes get you launching into a wrapping, rolling, dipping and feasting frenzy. Service is always friendly. (☎02-9557 1175; www.thanhbinh.com.au; 111 King St, Newtown; mains $18-28; �) 5-11pm Mon-Fri, noon-11pm Sat & Sun; ☒; ☒ Macdonaldtown)

Continental
DELI $$

21 🌐 MAP P90, B7

It's a pleasure to sit at the counter at this artfully-designed deli and snack on charcuterie and fish preserves while quaffing a glass of vermouth or a deeply-flavoured amaro. Staff look after you exceptionally well here. The bistro upstairs opens for dinner and weekend lunches and features inventive, well-presented dishes partly based on the deli fare. (☎02-8624 3131; www.continental delicatessen.com.au; 210 Australia St, Newtown; charcuterie $10-20; ☉noon-11pm Mon-Thu, to midnight Fri & Sat, to 10pm Sun; ☒Newtown)

Stinking Bishops
CHEESE $$

22 🌐 MAP P90, A7

A pungent array of artisanal cheeses is the raison d'être of this popular shop and eatery. Choose the varieties you want, pick a wine or craft beer to accompany, and off you go. There are also very tasty charcuterie boards. All its wares are sourced from small producers and available to take home too. (☎02-9007 7754; www.thestinkingbishops.com; 63 Enmore Rd, Newtown; 2-/3-/4-cheese boards

$21/29/37; ☉5-9pm Tue-Thu, noon-3.30pm & 5.30-10pm Fri & Sat; ☒; ☒Newtown)

Tramsheds Harold Park
FOOD HALL $$

23 🌐 MAP P90, B2

Sydney's latest foodie hangout is this refurbished centenarian brick tram depot at the northern end of Glebe. It's a handsome redevelopment with a supermarket, provedores and modern-thinking eateries, including one specialising in fresh pasta, another in organic meats, a sustainable fish restaurant, a contemporary Middle Eastern, a Spanishy tapas place from the Bodega team and Messina gelati. (☎02-8398 5695; www.tram shedssydney.com.au; Maxwell Rd, Glebe; ☉7am-10pm; ❄️ 🛜; ☒Jubilee Park)

Despaña
TAPAS $$

24 🌐 MAP P90, D3

Though service can be a little scatty, there's some excellent tapas-sharing to be done at this welcoming Glebe restaurant. A good selection of cured meats is backed up by full-of-flavour, loosely Spanish creations, with delicious artichokes, mushrooms and cauliflower dishes complemented by succulent lamb skewers, braised beef cheek and a selection of cheeses. The wine list covers both Spain and Argentina. (☎02-9660 2299; www.despana.com.au; 101 Glebe Point Rd, Glebe; tapas $9-18; ☉5-11pm Mon-Fri, noon-10pm Sat & Sun; ☒; 🚌431, 433, ☒Glebe)

Acre

MODERN AUSTRALIAN $$

25 MAP P90, B5

Part of Camperdown Commons, a conversion of a bowling club into organic farm and family-friendly cafe, eatery and play area, Acre is a breezy, good-looking, open-plan bungalow-style restaurant. Plenty of space between tables, tasty tap beers and excellent, carefully selected produce make this a pleasurable experience. The share plates of meat and fish are great. A shipping container out front serves coffee daily. (Camperdown Commons; ☎02-9194 3100; www.acreeatery.com.au; 31a Mallett St, Camperdown; mains $27-38; ⏲restaurant noon-10pm Wed-Sat, to 9pm Sun; 🛜👶)

Ester

MODERN AUSTRALIAN $$$

26 MAP P90, F5

Ester exemplifies Sydney's contemporary dining scene: informal but not sloppy; innovative without being overly gimmicky; hip, but never try-hard. Influences straddle continents and dishes are made to be shared. How do the dishes achieve that much flavour and texture? It's a seriously impressive place. If humanly possible, make room for dessert. (☎02-8068 8279; www.ester-restaurant.com.au; 46/52 Meagher St, Chippendale; share plates $18-50; ⏲6-10pm Mon-Thu, 6-11pm Fri, noon-3pm & 6-11pm Sat, noon-6pm Sun; 🅿; 🚆Central)

Changing Glebe

Glebe is home to a long-established Aboriginal community, students, academics, hipsters and cool bookstores. The First Fleet's chaplain was granted church land here (a 'glebe'); which later degenerated into slums. In the mid-1970s Gough Whitlam's federal government rejuvenated the area for low-income families, many of whom have lived here for generations. These days, though, you won't be low-income if you've just bought a pretty old terrace here.

Boathouse on Blackwattle Bay

SEAFOOD $$$

27 MAP P90, D1

The best restaurant in Glebe, and one of the best seafood restaurants in Sydney. Offerings range from oysters so fresh you'd think you shucked them yourself, to a snapper pie that'll go straight to the top of your favourite-dish list. The views over the bay and Anzac Bridge are stunning. Arrive by water taxi for maximum effect. (☎02-9518 9011; www.boathouse.net.au; 123 Ferry Rd, Glebe; mains $42-48; ⏲6-10pm Tue-Thu, noon-3pm & 6-11pm Fri-Sun; 🚆Glebe)

Glebe Point Diner

MODERN AUSTRALIAN $$$

28 MAP P90, C1

A sensational neighbourhood diner, where only the best local produce is used and everything – from the home-baked bread and hand-churned butter to the nougat finale – is made from scratch. The food is creative and comforting at the same time: a rare combination. The menu changes regularly and is backed up by blackboard specials. (02-9660 2646; www.glebepointdiner.com.au; 407 Glebe Point Rd, Glebe; mains $32; noon-3pm Wed-Sun, 6-10pm Mon-Thu, 5.30-11pm Fri & Sat; 431, Jubilee Park)

Drinking

Lazybones Lounge

BAR

29 MAP P90, A8

Roomy and extravagantly decorated, Lazybones is an excellent bar-lounge with live music nightly and a decent line in cocktails and food. At weekends it gets likeably louche, with a happy crowd dancing until late. Even the bouncers are friendly.

There's a cover charge for the bands ($10 to $20); it's free later on. Enter on Illawarra Rd. (0450 008 563; www.lazybones lounge.com.au; 294 Marrickville Rd, Marrickville; 7pm-midnight Mon-Wed, 5pm-3am Thu-Sat, 5-10pm Sun; ; Marrickville)

Earl's Juke Joint

BAR

30 MAP P90, B8

The current it-bar of the minute, swinging Earl's serves craft beers and killer cocktails to the Newtown hip-erati. It's hidden behind the down-at-heel facade of the butcher's shop it used to be, but once in, you're in swinging New Orleans, with a bar as long as the Mississippi. (www.facebook.com/earlsjukejoint; 407 King St, Newtown; 4pm-midnight Mon-Sat, 4-10pm Sun; Newtown)

Timbah

WINE BAR

31 MAP P90, C2

Quite a way down Glebe Point Rd is an excellent independent bottleshop; turn right to find this convivial wine bar it runs downstairs. It's a lovely space decked out in wood; there's always something interesting available by the glass, and staff are open to cracking something on demand. Tapas-style food (not Sundays) is tasty, with Australian native flavours and home-grown herbs. (02-9571 7005; www.timbahwinebar.com.au; 375 Glebe Point Rd, entrance on Forsyth St, Glebe; 4-10pm Tue-Thu, 4-11pm Fri & Sat, 4-8pm Sun; 431, Glebe)

Archie Rose Distilling Co.

BAR

32 MAP P90, F8

This distillery has made quite an impact with its excellent gins and where better to try them than the place itself? The bar is appropriately industrial chic;

the mezzanine is a great spot to sit and observe the action. Try different gins in a flight, or pick your perfect G&T combination or cocktail. It also has some decent wine and beer. (📞02-8458 2300; www.archierose.com.au; 85 Dunning Ave, Rosebery; 🕙noon-10pm Sun & Mon, to 11.30pm Tue-Sat; 🚇; 🚌343, 🚉Green Square)

The Henson PUB

33 🚇 MAP P90, A8

Offering something for everyone, this excellent neighbourhood pub sums up the modern Inner West vibe. Sip craft ale in various indoor spaces, watch charcuterie being sliced in the deli/beer shop or order up a plateful of delicious food. The beer garden sees a lot of action, and there's a great children's play area here, making it very popular with families. (📞02-9569 5858; www.thehenson.com.au; 91 Illawarra Rd, Marrickville; 🕙11am-midnight Mon-Sat, to 10pm Sun; 🚻; 🚌423, 426, 428, M30)

Gasoline Pony BAR

34 🚇 MAP P90, A8

With a friendly, 30-plus local crowd, this is an excellent bar with streetside seating, local live music and a relaxing backyard area if you don't fancy the sounds. The food is ok but you're here for the welcoming atmosphere and that Marrickville vibe. (📞02-9569 2668; www.gasolinepony.com; 115 Marrick-ville Rd, Marrickville; 🕙5-11.30pm Tue-Thu, 3-11.30pm Fri & Sat, 3-9.30pm Sun; 🚌418, 423, 425, 426, M30, 🚉Sydenham)

The butcher's-shop frontage of Earl's Juke Joint

Young Henry's
BREWERY

35  MAP P90, A7

Conviviality is assured in this craft brewery bar, where the beer is as fresh as you'll get. Basically, they've filled a bit of warehouse with high tables, a loud stereo system and a counter to serve their delicious beer, opened the roller door and filled it with happy locals. It doesn't do eats, but there's a different food truck outside each weekend. (02-9519 0048; www.younghenrys.com; 76 Wilford St, Newtown; noon-7pm; Newtown)

Courthouse Hotel
PUB

36 MAP P90, B7

A block back from the King St fray, the 150-year-old Courthouse is one of Newtown's best pubs, the kind of place where everyone from goth lesbians to magistrates can have a beer and feel right at home. It packs out for Sydney Swans games. The beer garden is one of Sydney's best: spacious, sheltered and cheerful, with decent pub food available. (02-9519 8273; www.solotel.com.au; 202 Australia St, Newtown; 10am-midnight Mon-Sat, to 10pm Sun; Newtown)

Erskineville Hotel
PUB

37 MAP P90, C7

The Erko's art-deco glory is something to behold, and it also happens to be one of the area's best pubs. The wood-lined beer garden, local characters, range of curious spaces to drink in, and good pub food served in generous portions makes it a real gem of the

Erskineville Hotel ('The Erko')

community. Unusually for Sydney pubs, it's even got some street-side tables. ([☎]02-9565 1608; www.theerko.com.au; 102 Erskineville Rd, Erskineville; [⏱]11am-midnight Mon-Sat, 11am-10pm Sun; [📶]; [🚉]Erskineville)

Hive Bar   BAR

38 [🚇] MAP P90, C8

In groovy Erskineville village, this breezy little corner bar lures the neighbourhood's hipsters with food, cocktails – try the Full Scottish Breakfast featuring marmalade and malt whisky – DJs spinning funk and soul, crazy murals and a quiet bolthole upstairs. Order a few plates to share over a glass of vino and pull up a footpath table. ([☎]02-9519 1376; www.thehivebar.com.au; 93 Erskineville Rd, Erskineville; [⏱]noon-midnight Mon-Fri, 11am-midnight Sat, 11am-10pm Sun; [📶]; [🚉]Erskineville)

Imperial Hotel   GAY & LESBIAN

39 [🚇] MAP P90, C7

The art-deco Imperial is legendary as the starting point for *The Adventures of Priscilla, Queen of the Desert*. This old, late-opening LGBTQ+ favourite put on a new frock in 2018, reopening with a mainly vegetarian restaurant and a refurbished basement space for the drag shows. ([☎]02-9516 1766; www.imperialerskineville.com.au; 35 Erskineville Rd, Erskineville; [⏱]noon-midnight Mon-Thu, noon-3am Fri & Sat, 11am-midnight Sun; [🚉]Erskineville)

Sly Fox   PUB

40 [🚇] MAP P90, A7

This late-opener kicks off its week on Wednesdays with Birdcage, one of Sydney's key lesbian nights. Over the weekend it features live music and DJs taking up the baton until everyone's booted out into the dawn. ([☎]02-9557 2917; www.slyfox.sydney; 199 Enmore Rd, Enmore; [⏱]6pm-3am Wed & Thu, to 6am Fri & Sat; [🚌]423, 426, 428, M30)

Bank Hotel   PUB

41 [🚇] MAP P90, B7

The Bank didn't always sport the artful heritage-wood look that it has now, but it has consistently been a Newtown classic in its central railway-side position. Its large retractable-roofed beer garden at the back is a highlight, as is the craft beer bar above it, which always has interesting guest ales on tap. Food is based on Mexican-style barbecue options. ([☎]02-8568 1900; www.bankhotel.com.au; 324 King St, Newtown; [⏱]11am-1am Mon-Wed, to 2am Thu, to 4am Fri & Sat, to midnight Sun; [📶]; [🚉]Newtown)

Marlborough Hotel   PUB

42 [🚇] MAP P90, C6

One of many great old art-deco pubs in Newtown, the Marly has a front sports bar with live bands on weekends and a shady beer garden. Head upstairs for a great balcony, soul food and rockabilly bands at Miss Peaches, or downstairs for all sorts of kooky happenings at the Tokyo Sing Song nightclub on Friday and Saturday nights. (📞02-9519 1222; www.marlboroughhotel.com.au; 145 King St, Newtown; ⏰10am-4am Mon-Sat, 10am-midnight Sun; 🚉Macdonaldtown)

Friend in Hand PUB

43 🚶 MAP P90, E3

At heart the Friend in Hand is still a working-class pub with a resident loud-mouth cockatoo and a cast of grizzly old-timers and local larrikins propping up the bar. But then there's all the other stuff: live music, life drawing, poetry readings, crab racing, comedy nights. Strewth Beryl, bet you weren't expecting that. (📞02-9660 2326; www.friendinhand.com.au; 58 Cowper St, Glebe; ⏰8am-midnight Mon-Fri, 10am-midnight Sat, 10am-10pm Sun; 📶; 🚉Wentworth Park)

Entertainment

Bald Faced Stag LIVE MUSIC

44 ⭐ MAP P90, A5

One of Sydney's oldest pubs, the Stag is a friendly, down-to-earth place with pool tables and a beer garden. New owners have really ramped up the live-music scene here, with regular gigs in a dedicated space that tend to be at the heavier end of the spectrum. It's a cracking spot. (📞02-9560 7188; www.baldfacedstag.com.au; 345 Parramatta Rd, Leichhardt; ⏰11am-1am Mon-Thu, to 3am Fri & Sat, to 10pm Sun; 🚌413, 436-440, 444, 461, 480, 483, M10)

Leadbelly LIVE MUSIC

45 ⭐ MAP P90, C6

This dark and atmospheric bar does seriously good cocktails and some excellent jazz and blues-y live music at weekends. There are also pizzas and other food, so that's your whole night sorted. (📞02-9557 7992; www.theleadbelly.com.au; 42 King St, Newtown; ⏰6pm-midnight Tue-Thu, 6pm-1am Fri & Sat; 🚌352, 370, 422, 423, 426, 428, M30, M30; 🚉Macdonaldtown)

Camelot Lounge LIVE MUSIC

46 ⭐ MAP P90, A8

In increasingly hip Marrickville, this eclectic little venue hosts jazz, world music, blues, folk, comedy, cabaret and all manner of other weird stuff. There are two bars; it's worth booking online or getting here early as it often sells out. The atmosphere is one of sit-down-and-appreciate rather than stand and dance. It's very close to Sydenham station. Check the website for shows outside open nights. (📞02-9550 3777; www.camelotlounge.com; 19 Marrickville Rd, Marrickville; ⏰6pm-late Thu-Sun; 🚉Sydenham)

Lansdowne Hotel LIVE MUSIC

47 ⭐ MAP P90, E4

This famous Sydney venue is back in action after a period of closure. It's a likeably no-frills rock pub downstairs, with graffiti on the walls and food served until 2am. Upstairs, there are gigs most nights; prepare for around $20 cover charge at weekends, depending on the band(s). (📞02-8218 2333; www.thelansdownepub.com.au; 2 City Rd, Chippendale; 🕐noon-3am Mon-Sat, to midnight Sun; 🚌412, 413, 422, 423, 🚆Central)

Foundry 616   LIVE MUSIC

48 ⭐ **MAP P90, F3**

With live Australian and international contemporary jazz several times a week, this atmospheric and thoughtfully programmed venue has been a great shot in the arm for the Sydney live-music scene. Good-value meals are available if you want a table. (📞02-9211 9442; www.foundry616.com.au; 616

Harris St, Ultimo; 🚋Paddy's Markets, 🚆Central)

Shopping

Carriageworks
Farmers Market   MARKET

Over 70 regular stallholders sell their goodies at Sydney's best farmers market (see 4 ◉ Map p90, D6), held in a heritage-listed railway workshop (p92). Food and coffee stands do a brisk business and vegetables, fruit, meat and seafood from all over the state are sold in a convivial atmosphere. (http://carriageworks.com.au; Carriageworks, 245 Wilson St, Eveleigh; 🕐8am-1pm Sat; 🚆Redfern)

Camelot Lounge

Mitchell Road Antique & Design Centre

ANTIQUES, VINTAGE

49 🔒 MAP P90, E8

This extraordinary vintage and antique market is a warehouse full of retro chic, whether you are after original 1970s Lego, pre-loved rocking horses, a Georgian coronation tea set or Bakelite telephones. For some it will be a dive into a past known only from movies, for others a trip down memory lane. (☎02-9698 0907; https://mitchellroad.word press.com; 17 Bourke Rd, Alexandria; ⏰10am-6pm; 🚉Green Square)

Little Bottleshop

WINE

One of Sydney's best bottleshops for those interested in Australian wine, this unassuming place (see 31 Map p90, C2) features an excellent curated selection of small-vineyard wines from quality regions. Look out for their own 2037 (Glebe's postcode) bottlings. It runs a wine bar (p100) downstairs. (Glebe Liquor; ☎02-9660 1984; www.glebeliquor. com.au; 375 Glebe Point Rd, Glebe; ⏰10am-8pm Mon-Sat, to 7pm Sun; 🚌431, 🚉Glebe)

Gleebooks

BOOKS

50 🔒 MAP P90, D3

One of Sydney's best bookshops, Gleebooks' aisles are full of politics, arts and general fiction, and staff really know their stuff. Check its calendar for author talks and book launches. (☎02-9660 2333; www.gleebooks.com.au; 49 Glebe Point Rd, Glebe; ⏰9am-7pm Mon-Sat, 10am-6pm Sun; 🚌431, 433, 🚉Glebe)

Antique cash register, Mitchell Road Antique & Design Centre

Better Read Than Dead

BOOKS

51 🔒 MAP P90, B7

This is our favourite Newtown bookshop, and not just because of the pithy name and the great selection of Lonely Planet titles. Nobody seems to mind if you waste hours perusing the beautifully presented aisles, stacked with high-, middle- and deliciously low-brow reading materials. (☏02-9557 8700; www.betterread. com.au; 265 King St, Newtown; ⊙9.30am-9pm Sun-Wed, to 10pm Thu-Sat; 🚇Newtown)

Deus Ex Machina

FASHION & ACCESSORIES

52 🔒 MAP P90, B4

This kooky showroom is crammed with classic and custom-made motorcycles and surfboards. A hybrid workshop, cafe and offbeat boutique, it stocks men's and women's threads, including Deus-branded jeans, tees and shorts. (☏02-8594 2800; www.deuscustoms. com; 102-104 Parramatta Rd, Camperdown; ⊙9am-5pm Mon-Fri, 10am-4pm Sat & Sun; 🚌436-440)

Glebe Markets

MARKET

53 🔒 MAP P90, D4

The best of the west: Sydney's hipster inner-city contingent beats a course to this crowded retro-chic market. There are some great

Updated Alexandria

The warehouses of Alexandria, at one time Australia's largest industrial district, were once the unflattering first glimpse that many visitors got of Sydney as their cab drove them from airport to city. These days, though, there's all sorts going on in this up-and-coming area. Groundbreaking cafes, smart food culture, renovated pubs, creative industries and a range of outlet stores make it well worth discovering. Note that the distance between reconstructed areas makes cycling a good option here.

handcrafts and design on sale, as well as an inclusive, community atmosphere. (www.glebemarkets. com.au; Glebe Public School, cnr Glebe Point Rd & Derby Pl; ⊙10am-4pm Sat; 🚌431, 433, 🚇Glebe)

Revolve Records

MUSIC

54 🔒 MAP P90, C8

Vinyl hounds should head here, just up from Erskineville station for a treasure-trove of second-hand records of all types. (☏02-9519 9978; www.revolverecords.com. au; 65 Erskineville Rd, Erskineville; ⊙noon-6pm Mon-Wed, 11.30am-7pm Thu & Fri, 10am-6pm Sat & Sun; 🚇Erskineville)

Walking Tour 🚶

A Saturday in Paddington

Paddington is an elegant neighbourhood of restored terrace houses and steep leafy streets where fashionable folks (seemingly without the need to occupy an office) drift between boutiques, art galleries and bookshops. The suburb's pulsing artery is Oxford St, built over an ancient track used by the Gadigal (Cadigal) people. The liveliest time to visit is on Saturday, when the markets are effervescing.

Getting There

🚌 Buses 333 (Circular Quay to North Bondi) and 380 (Circular Quay to Watsons Bay via Bondi) head along Oxford St. Bus 389 (Maritime Museum to Bondi Junction) takes the back roads.

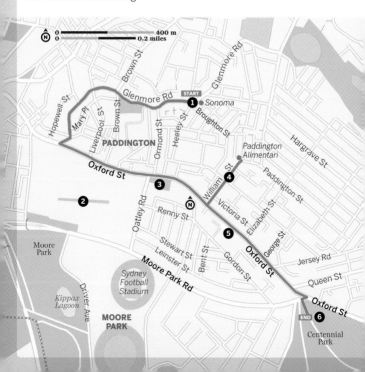

❶ Hang out in Five Ways

Oxford St may be the main drag, but the quirky cafes, galleries, shops and pub at the star-like junction of **Five Ways** (Glenmore Rd, Paddington; 🚌389) make it the hip heart of Paddington. Start with coffee in **Sonoma** (📞02-9331 3601; www.sonoma.com.au; 241 Glenmore Rd, Paddington; mains $6-18; ⏱7am-3pm Mon-Sat, 7am-2pm Sun; 🛜; 🚌389), a bakery-cafe specialising in sourdough bread and popular with the yummy-mummy set.

❷ Peer at Victoria Barracks

A manicured vision from the peak of the British Empire, these Georgian **barracks** (📞02-8335 5170; www.armymuseumnsw.com.au; Oxford St, Paddington; admission free; ⏱tours 10am Thu; 🚌333, 352, 380, 440, M40), built 1841-48, have been called the finest of their kind in the colonies. They're still part of an army base, so unless you return for the tour you'll have to peer through the gates.

❸ Stroll Through Paddington Reservoir Gardens

This impressive **park** (cnr Oxford St & Oatley Rd, Paddington; 🚌333, 352, 380, 440, M40) makes use of Paddington's long-abandoned 1866 water reservoir, incorporating the brick arches and surviving chamber into an interesting green space featuring a sunken garden, pond, boardwalk and lawns. They've even preserved some of the graffiti.

❹ Wander Down William St

William Street is an achingly pretty little slope whose cute terraced houses have been converted into upmarket clothing boutiques. It's a marvellous stroll; at the bottom, **Paddington Alimentari** (📞02-9358 2142; www.facebook.com/paddington.alimentari; 2 Hopetoun St, Paddington; light meals $5-13; ⏱7am-5pm Mon-Fri, 7.30am-4pm Sat; 🚌333, 352, 380, 440, M40) is a great cafe-deli that's an essential stop for local residents.

❺ Experience Paddington Markets

A cultural experience, these quirky, long-running **markets** (📞02-9331 2923; www.paddingtonmarkets.com.au; 395 Oxford St, Paddington; ⏱10am-4pm Sat; 🚌333, 380) turn Saturdays in Paddington into pandemonium. In the 1970s, when they started, Paddington Markets were distinctly counter-cultural. It's a tad more mainstream now, but still worth checking out for new and vintage clothing, crafts, jewellery, food and holistic treatments.

❻ Explore Centennial Park

Sydney's biggest **park** (📞02-9339 6699; www.centennialparklands.com.au; Oxford St, Centennial Park; ⏱gates sunrise-sunset; 🚊Moore Park, 🚉Bondi Junction) is a rambling 189-hectare expanse full of horse riders, joggers, cyclists and in-line skaters. Among the wide formal avenues, ponds and statues is the domed Federation Pavilion – the spot where Australia was officially proclaimed a nation.

Explore ◈
Surry Hills & Darlinghurst

Sydney's hippest and gayest neighbourhood is also home to its most interesting dining and bar scene. The plane trees and up-and-down of chic Surry Hills merge into the terraces of vibrant Darlinghurst. They are pleasant, leafy districts appealingly close to the centre.

Surry Hills bears little resemblance these days to the tightly knit, working-class community so evocatively documented in Ruth Park's classic Depression-era novels set here. The rows of Victorian terrace houses remain, but they're now upmarket residences home to inner-city types who keep the many excellent neighbourhood restaurants and bars in business.

Adjacent Darlinghurst is synonymous with Sydney's vibrant and visible gay community. Oxford St has traditionally been Sydney's sequinned mile, and while it's seen better days it's still home to most of the city's dwindling gay venues and the Mardi Gras parade.

Getting There & Around

🚆 Exit at Museum train station for East Sydney and the blocks around Oxford St; Central for the rest of Surry Hills; and Kings Cross for the northern and eastern reaches of Darlinghurst.

🚌 Numerous buses traverse Cleveland, Crown, Albion, Oxford, Liverpool and Flinders Sts.

🚈 In 2019, Sydney's second light-rail line will open with a stop in southern Surry Hills.

Surry Hills & Darlinghurst Map on p114

Top Sight 📷
Australian Museum

Under ongoing modernisation, this four-square sandstone museum, established just 40 years after the First Fleet dropped anchor, is doing a brilliant job. As well as natural history exhibits, it covers Indigenous Australia, dinosaurs, minerals and more.

◉ **MAP P114, C1**

☏ 02-9320 6000

www.australianmuseum.
net.au

6 College St, Darlinghurst

adult/child $15/free

🕑 9.30am-5pm

🚍 Museum

Long Gallery

This elegant two-level space focuses on 100 key objects from the museum's extensive collection (from a platypus-skin rug to an Egyptian death-boat to the 'Bone Ranger', a spooky skeletal horserider) and, upstairs, 100 key Australians including household names and some who should be far better known.

Indigenous Galleries

Australia's Indigenous past and present gets good treatment in this standout section covering Aboriginal history and spirituality, from Dreaming stories to videos of the Freedom Rides of the 1960s. A collection of art and artefacts provides further insights.

Creatures

The excellent dinosaur gallery is a sure hit with kids and adults alike. Among several imposing beasts, it features enormous Jobaria as well as local bruisers like Muttaburrasaurus.

The stuffed-animal gallery of the natural history section manages to keep it relevant, while there are also interesting displays on extinct megafauna (giant wombats – simultaneously cuddly and terrifying) and current Australian creatures.

The Pacific

An intriguing collection of objects from a range of Pacific cultures is a real dose of colour and life after the stuffed animals. It's an assemblage of great quality that will at some point be incorporated into a new Oceania display.

★ **Top Tips**

o Kidspace on level 2 is a mini-museum for the under-fives.

o Even if you're not hungry, don't miss heading up to the cafe, which has brilliant views of St Mary's Cathedral and down to Woolloomooloo.

✗ **Take a Break**

The museum **cafe** is a fine spot for a snack and a drink with vistas.

Nearby Stanley Street still has a few remnants of its Little Italy heyday. **Bar Reggio** (☏ 02-9332 1129; www.barreggio. com.au; 135 Crown St, Darlinghurst; mains $14-30; ⊗ noon-11pm Mon-Sat; ☞; ☒ Museum), just round the corner, is one of the most typical.

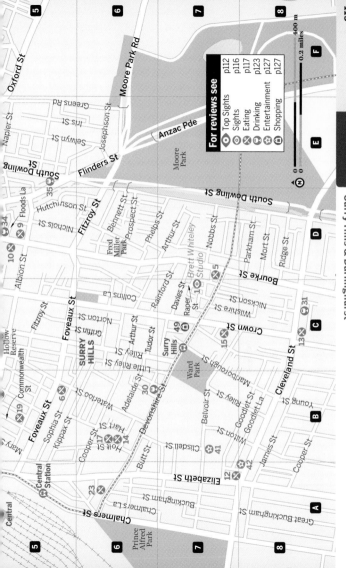

Surry Hills & Darlinghurst

For reviews see

◎	Top Sights	p112
◉	Sights	p116
✕	Eating	p117
◻	Drinking	p123
✪	Entertainment	p127
◻	Shopping	p127

100 m
0.2 miles

Sights

Brett Whiteley Studio   GALLERY

1 ◎ MAP P114, C7

Acclaimed local artist Brett Whiteley (1939–1992) lived fast and without restraint. His hard-to-find studio (look for the signs on Devonshire St) has been preserved as a gallery for some of his best work. Pride of place goes to his astonishing *Alchemy,* a giant multi-panel extravaganza that could absorb you for hours with its broad themes, intricate details and humorous asides. The studio room upstairs also gives great insight into the character of this masterful draughtsman and off-the-wall genius.

At the door is a miniature of his famous sculpture *Almost Once,* which you can see in all its glory in the Domain. (☏02-9225 1881; www.artgallery.nsw.gov.au/brett-whiteley-studio; 2 Raper St, Surry Hills; admission free; ⏱10am-4pm Fri-Sun; ⛾Surry Hills, ⛊Central)

Sydney Jewish Museum   MUSEUM

2 ◎ MAP P114, E3

This recently revamped museum revolves around a detailed and expertly curated exhibition on the Holocaust, with sobering personal testimonies and moving objects as well as a memorial section for the 1.5 million child victims. Other sections cover the history and practice of Judaism itself and Australian Jewish history, culture and tradition.

Another examines the role of Jews in Australia's military, while temporary exhibitions are always excellent. There's a kosher cafe upstairs.

Sydney has had an important Jewish history from the time of the First Fleet (which included 16 known Jews), to the immediate aftermath of WWII (when Australia became home to the greatest number of Holocaust survivors per capita, after Israel), to the present day. Visiting on a Sunday or weekday afternoon is recommended, as the museum often packs out with school groups. (☏02-9360 7999; www.sydneyjewishmuseum.com.au; 148 Darlinghurst Rd, Darlinghurst; adult/teen/child $15/9/free; ⏱10am-4pm Sun-Thu, to 2pm Fri; ⛊Kings Cross)

National Art School   HISTORIC SITE, GALLERY

3 ◎ MAP P114, E3

Until 1912 these sandstone buildings were Darlinghurst Gaol: writer Henry Lawson was repeatedly incarcerated here for debt (he called the place 'Starvinghurst'). If today's art students think they've got it tough, they should spare a thought for the 732 prisoners crammed in here, or the 76 who were hanged. The central circular building was the chapel. A tiny former morgue near the Burton St exit has creepy skull-and-crossbone carvings. There's also a cafe and an excellent on-site gallery showcasing students' work. (www.nas.edu.au; Forbes St, Darlinghurst; admission free; ⏱gallery 11am-5pm Mon-Sat; ⛊Kings Cross)

Australian Design Centre

GALLERY

4 MAP P114, D1

The non-profit Australian Design Centre has a gallery, Object, that presents innovative exhibitions of new craft and design from Australia and overseas. Furniture, fashion, textiles and glass are all on show, and there's an appealing shop. (☏02-9361 4555; www.object.com.au; 101 William St, Darlinghurst; admission free; ⊙11am-4pm Tue-Sat; ☒Museum)

Eating

Bourke Street Bakery

BAKERY $

5 MAP P114, D7

Queuing outside this teensy bakery is an essential Surry Hills experience. It sells a tempting selection of pastries, cakes, bread and sandwiches, along with sausage rolls that are near legendary in these parts. There are a few tables inside but on a fine day you're better off on the street. Offshoots around town offer a bit more space. (☏02-9699 1011; www.bourkestreetbakery.com.au; 633 Bourke St, Surry Hills; items $5-14; ⊙7am-6pm Mon-Fri, to 5pm Sat & Sun; ☒; ☒301, ☒Surry Hills, ☒Central)

Le Monde

CAFE $

6 MAP P114, B5

Some of Sydney's best breakfasts are served between the demure dark wooden walls of this small street-side cafe. Top-notch coffee and a terrific selection of tea will gear you up to face the world, while dishes such as truffled

Entrance to the National Art School

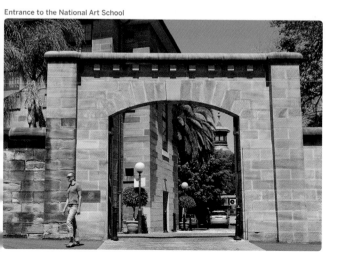

poached eggs or confit pork belly make it worth walking up the hill for. (📞02-9211 3568; www.lemonde cafe.com.au; 83 Foveaux St, Surry Hills; dishes $10-16; ⏲6.30am-4pm Mon-Fri, 7am-2pm Sat; 🛜; 🚉Central)

Reuben Hills
CAFE $

7 🆇 MAP P114, B5

An industrial fitout and Latin American menu await here at Reuben Hills (aka hipster central), set in a terrace and its former garage. Fantastic single-origin coffee, roasted on the premises, and fried chicken, but the eggs, tacos and *baleadas* (Honduran tortillas) are no slouches, either. (📞02-9211 5556; www.reubenhills.com.au; 61 Albion St, Surry Hills; mains $9-22; ⏲7am-4pm Mon-Sat, 7.30am-4pm Sun; 🛜🚭; 🚉Central)

The Surry Scene

Once upon a time, this neighbourhood was known for its grungy live-music pubs and high-octane gay scene. Many of the music venues have subsequently been converted into chic bar-restaurants and the gay bars have dwindled, but this area still contains some of Sydney's best nightspots – you just have to look harder to find them. The 'small bar' phenomenon has taken off here, with many of he city's best lurking down the most unlikely lanes.

Messina
ICE CREAM $

8 🆇 MAP P114, F2

Join the queues of people who look like they never eat ice cream at the counter of the original store of Sydney's most popular gelato shop. Clearly even the beautiful people can't resist quirky flavours such as figs in marsala and pannacotta with fig jam and amaretti biscuit. It's all delicious, and there are several dairy-free options. There are several more outlets around town now.

Book well ahead for the sumptuous $130-a-head dessert degustations that they put on at one table next door. (📞02-9331 1588; www.gelatomessina.com; 241 Victoria St, Darlinghurst; 1/2/3 scoops $4.80/6.80/8.80; ⏲noon-11pm Sun-Thu, to 11.30pm Fri & Sat; 🚭; 🚉Kings Cross)

Gratia
CAFE $

9 🆇 MAP P114, D5

This great cafe, Gratia, with genuinely friendly staff and a pleasant, light feel, does juices and eclectic brunchy fare. Like its restaurant section, Folonomo (p120), all profits are donated to charities, which customers can help choose. There's a gallery space upstairs too, and it actively helps and trains refugees. (📞02-8034 3818; www. gratia.org.au; 372 Bourke St, Surry Hills; dishes $10-19; ⏲8am-3pm Tue-Sun Oct-Mar, Thu-Sun Apr-Sep; 🛜🚭; 🚌374, 397, 399)

Formaggi Ocello

CAFE $

10   MAP P114, D5

Love a cheesy grin? Then Formaggi Ocello is for you. This excellent Italian deli has a great range of cheeses, mostly Italian, Spanish and French, with some top Aussie selections, too. Check out the humongous cheese wheels in the ageing room. It's also a great place for a panino or tasting platter, accompanied by a glass of wine or two. (☎02-9357 7878; www.ocello. com.au; 425 Bourke St, Surry Hills; light meals $8-16; ☏10am-6pm Mon-Fri, 9am-6pm Sat; 🖪; 🚃Central)

Spice I Am

THAI $

11   MAP P114, B3

Once the preserve of expat Thais, this little red-hot chilli pepper now has queues out the door. No wonder, as everything we've tried from the 70-plus dishes on the menu is superfragrant and superspicy. It's been so successful that it's opened the upmarket version in **Darlinghurst** (☎02-9332 2445; 296-300 Victoria St, Darlinghurst; mains $19-24; ☏5-10pm; 🖪; 🚃Kings Cross). The sign is very unobtrusive so it's easy to walk past: don't. (☎02-9280 0928; www.spiceiam.com; 90 Wentworth Ave, Surry Hills; mains $15-20; ☏11.30am-3.30pm & 5-10pm Tue-Sun; 🖪; 🚃Central)

Nada's

LEBANESE $

12   MAP P114, A7

There are swisher Lebanese restaurants around, but for a no-frills delicious feed at a very fair price, it's hard to beat this old family-run favourite. The set meal at $29 a head is a bargain; just don't fill up too much on the bread and dips or you won't manage the sizeable chunks of Turkish delight at the end. BYO with no corkage. (☎02-9690 1289; www.nadasrestaurant.com; 270 Cleveland St, Surry Hills; mains $13-16; ☏noon-2.30pm & 6-10pm Wed-Mon, 6-10pm Tue; 🖪; 🚃372, 🚃Central)

Erciyes

TURKISH $

13   MAP P114, C8

Shamelessly kitsch Erciyes flaunts its fluoro lighting, mirror-faced wall, plastic tablecloths, disco ball and audience-participatory belly-dancing on Friday and Saturday nights. It's a well-loved spot that's been around for yonks: a good-value, good-time Turkish eatery. It has a few wine options, but it's also BYO. (☎02-9319 1309; www.erciyes restaurant.com.au; 409 Cleveland St, Surry Hills; mains $15-26; ☏11am-11.30pm; 🖪; 🚃372, 393, 395)

Porteño

ARGENTINE $$

14   MAP P114, B6

This upbeat and deservedly acclaimed Argentine restaurant is a great place to eat. The 'animal of the day' is slow-roasted for eight hours before the doors even open and is always delicious. Other highlights include the homemade chorizo and morcilla, but lighter touches are also in evidence, so it's not all meat-feast. There's a decent Argentine wine list too. (☎02-8399

1440; www.porteno.com.au; 50 Holt St, Surry Hills; sharing plates $20-50; ⏱6pm-midnight Tue-Sat, plus noon-3pm Fri; 🚇Central)

Folonomo
MODERN AUSTRALIAN $$

Not-for-profit eateries often score higher on good intentions than cooking, but this one (see 9  Map p114, D5) is the real deal. Folonomo (from 'for love not money') serves brilliant modern Australian fare, with seasonally changing menus, in a bohemian, exposed-brick space next to their cafe, Gratia (p118). All profits go to charitable organisations, which diners can help choose. Applause. (📞02-8034 3818; www.folonomo.org.au; 370 Bourke St, Surry Hills; large plates $15-32; ⏱6-10.30pm Tue-Sun; 🛜📶; 🚌374, 397, 399)

Bishop Sessa
BISTRO $$

15 ❌ MAP P114, C7

Reviving the disappearing Sydney tradition of shopfront-style restaurants in terraced houses, this two-level European-influenced spot offers quality bistro eating at very acceptable prices for stylish Surry Hills. Home-made charcuterie, decent wine choices and appealingly presented and executed seafood, meat and pasta dishes make this a reliably good choice. You'll feel a world away from the busy Sydney street corner photo featured upstairs. (📞02-8065 7223; www.bishopsessa. com.au; 527 Crown St, Surry Hills; 2/3 courses $49/59, degustation $77; ⏱noon-11pm Tue-Sat; 🚇Surry Hills)

Meat pie from the Bourke Street Bakery (p117)

Baccomatto Osteria ITALIAN $$

16 MAP P114, C3

Sleek and modern, this smart Italian restaurant nevertheless conserves the warm and genuine welcome of your favourite trattoria. There's a real verve to the updated but faithful Italian cooking and some extraordinary flavours. The $20 pasta-and-wine lunches are a top deal. (02-9215 5140; www.baccomattoosteria.com.au; 212 Riley St, Surry Hills; mains $29-35; 6-10pm Mon-Thu, noon-3pm & 6-10pm Fri-Sun; 301-2, 352)

Muum Maam THAI $$

17 MAP P114, B6

Packing a punch for eyes and taste-buds, this is a buzzy spot beloved of those creative types who work hereabouts. It has a double identity that really works, with a food cart doling out lunch specials before the open kitchen turns to more serious, lavishly presented Thai creations in the evening. There's a big communal table but you can also go solo. (02-9318 0881; www.muummaam.com.au; 50 Holt St, Surry Hills; lunch dishes $14-16, dinner mains $18-32; 11.30am-3pm & 6-10.30pm Mon-Fri, 6-10.30pm Sat; Central)

Single O CAFE $

18 MAP P114, B4

Unshaven graphic designers roll cigarettes at little outdoor tables in the bricky hollows of Surry Hills, while inside impassioned, bouncing-off-the-walls caffeine fiends prepare their beloved brews, along with a tasty selection of cafe fare. Something of a trendsetter a few years back, this place still does coffee as good as anywhere in Sydney. The hole-in-the-wall alongside does takeaways. (Single Origin Roasters; 02-9211 0665; www.singleo.com.au; 60-64 Reservoir St, Surry Hills; mains $14-23; 6.30am-4pm Mon-Fri, 7.30am-3pm Sat, 8am-3pm Sun; Central)

Bodega TAPAS $$

19 MAP P114, B5

The coolest progeny of Sydney's tapas explosion, Bodega has a casual vibe, good-lookin' staff and a funky matador mural. Dishes vary widely in size and price and are very loosely rooted in Central American and Spanish cuisine. Wash 'em down with Spanish and South American wine, sherry, port or beer, and plenty of Latin gusto. (02-9212 7766; www.bodegatapas.com; 216 Commonwealth St, Surry Hills; tapas $12-24, share plates $20-32; noon-2pm Fri, 6-10pm Tue-Sat; Central)

Chaco JAPANESE $$

20 MAP P114, D3

This little place has a simple, effortless Japanese cool and some seriously good food. The ramen are good, and there are very succulent gyoza and delicious meatball sticks to dip in egg. The yakitori skewers are available Tuesday to Saturday nights and are a highlight, bursting with flavour.

Don't be afraid to try the more unusual ones. (☏02-9007 8352; www.chacobar.com.au; 238 Crown St, Darlinghurst; skewers $4-9; ⏱ramen 5.30-9pm Mon, 11.30am-2.30pm Wed-Sun, yakitori 5.30-10pm Tue-Sat; ☒Museum)

Dead Ringer
TAPAS $$

21 ✕ MAP P114, D4

This charcoal-fronted terrace is a haven of quality eating and drinking in a laid-back format. Barstool it or grab an outdoor table and graze on the short menu that changes slightly daily and runs from bar snacks through tapas to mains. Though well-presented, the food's all about flavour combinations rather than airy artistry. There's always something interesting by the glass to accompany. (☏02-9331 3560; http://deadringer.wtf; 413 Bourke St, Surry Hills; dishes $18-37; ⏱4-11pm Mon-Thu, 4pm-midnight Fri, 11am-midnight Sat, 11am-11pm Sun; 🛜🍴; 🚌333, 380, 440)

Bar H
ASIAN $$

22 ✕ MAP P114, B3

Marrying Chinese and Japanese dishes with native Australian bush ingredients, this sexy, shiny, black-walled corner eatery is unique and extremely impressive. Dishes range considerably in size and are designed to be shared; confer with your waiter about quantities. There's an $88 tasting menu that offers a fine experience of the quality and diversity on offer.

(☏02-9280 1980; www.barhsurryhills.com; 80 Campbell St, Surry Hills; dishes $14-39; ⏱6-10pm Mon-Thu, 5-11pm Fri & Sat; 🚇Central)

Devon
CAFE $

23 ✕ MAP P114, A6

If it's boring old bacon and eggs you're after, look elsewhere. Devon energetically fuses the cuisines of multicultural Australia to deliver an extremely creative menu, with plenty of twists on old favourites and things like pork belly and miso salmon popping up on the menu. It doesn't look like much from the street, but has a pleasant back courtyard area. (☏02-9211 8777; www.devoncafe.com.au; 76 Devonshire St, Surry Hills; dishes $14-24; ⏱7am-3.30pm Mon-Fri, 8am-3.30pm Sat & Sun; 🛜; 🚇Central)

Firedoor
GRILL $$$

24 ✕ MAP P114, B4

All the dishes in this moodily attractive sunken space are produced over a blazing fire, chef Lennox Hastie matching different woods to the flavours of meat, seafood and vegetables to create extraordinary dishes with huge depth of flavour. The menu changes on a daily basis and always intrigues. (☏02-8204 0800; www.firedoor.com.au; 33 Mary St, Surry Hills; mains $25-67, degustation $90; ⏱5.30-11pm Tue, Wed & Sat, noon-3pm & 5.30-11pm Thu & Fri; 🚇Central)

Nomad

MEDITERRANEAN $$$

25 MAP P114, B3

Though this large open space has a modern industrial look, with exposed surfaces and visible ducting, the cuisine takes its inspiration from more traditional vectors. Excellent share options apply old-school techniques like pickling and marinating to a range of ingredients, creating Mediterranean masterpieces with soul. Kick things off with house charcuterie; ask for some fresh-baked focaccia bread to accompany it.

The all-Australian wine list is short but has some super small-vineyard gems on it. (02-9280 3395; www.nomadwine.com.au; 16 Foster St, Surry Hills; share plates $25-48; noon-2.30pm & 5.30-10pm Mon-Sat; Central)

Red Lantern on Riley

VIETNAMESE $$$

26 MAP P114, D1

This atmospheric eatery is run by television presenters Luke Nguyen (*Luke Nguyen's Vietnam* and others), Mark Jensen (*Ready Steady Cook*) and sister/wife Pauline Nguyen (author of the excellent *Secrets of the Red Lantern* cookbook-cum-autobiography). It serves modern takes on classic Vietnamese dishes. (02-9698 4355; www.redlantern.com.au; 60 Riley St, Darlinghurst; mains $38-45; 6-10pm Sun-Thu, noon-3pm & 6-11pm Fri, 6-11pm Sat; ; Museum)

Longrain

THAI $$$

27 MAP P114, B3

Devotees flock to this century-old, wedge-shaped printing-press building to feast on fragrant modern Thai dishes, and to sip delicately flavoured and utterly delicious cocktails. Sit at shared tables or more private booths. (02-9280 2888; www.longrain.com; 85 Commonwealth St, Surry Hills; mains $24-36; 6-11pm Mon-Thu, noon-2.30pm & 6pm-midnight Fri, 5.30pm-midnight Sat & Sun; ; Central)

Drinking

Love, Tilly Devine

WINE BAR

28 MAP P114, D1

This dark and good-looking split-level laneway bar is pretty compact, but the wine list certainly isn't. It's an extraordinary document, with some exceptionally well-chosen wines and a mission to get people away from their tried-and-tested favourites and explore. Take a friend and crack open a leisurely bottle of something. Italian deli bites and fuller plates are on hand too. (02-9326 9297; www.lovetillydevine.com; 91 Crown Lane, Darlinghurst; 5pm-midnight Mon-Sat, to 10pm Sun; Museum)

Wild Rover

BAR

29 MAP P114, B3

Look for the unsigned wide door and enter this supremely cool brick-lined speakeasy, where a big range of craft beer is served in chrome steins and jungle animals peer benevolently from the green walls. The upstairs bar opens for trivia and live bands. (☎02-9280 2235; www.thewildrover.com.au; 75 Campbell St, Surry Hills; ☺4pm-midnight Mon-Sat; ▣Central)

Shakespeare Hotel PUB

30 🚇 MAP P114, B6

This is a classic Sydney pub (1879) with art-nouveau tiled walls, skuzzy carpet, the horses on the TV and cheap bar meals. There are plenty of cosy hidey-holes upstairs and a cast of local characters. It's a proper convivial all-welcome place that's the antithesis of the more gentrified Surry Hills drinking establishments. (☎02-9319 6883; www.shakespearehotel.com.au; 200 Devonshire St, Surry Hills; ☺10am-midnight Mon-Sat, 11am-10pm Sun; ▣Surry Hills, ▣Central)

Vasco COCKTAIL BAR

31 🚇 MAP P114, C8

Like the much, much hipper and better-looking Italian cousin of a Hard Rock Cafe, Vasco serves beer, wine and rock-themed cocktails in a room lined with band photos and with a Dave Grohl guitar on the wall. Order a plate of salumi or homemade gnocchi to snack on as you sip your creation, while Jagger pouts on the screen. (☎0406 775 436; www.vascobar.com; 421 Cleveland St, Redfern; ☺5pm-midnight Mon-Sat; 🛜; 🚌372)

Shady Pines Saloon BAR

32 🚇 MAP P114, D3

With no sign or street number on the door and entry via a shady back lane (look for the white door before Bikram Yoga on Foley St), this subterranean honky-tonk bar caters to the urban boho. Sip whisky and rye with the good ole hipster boys amid Western memorabilia and taxidermy. (www.shadypinessaloon.com; 4/256 Crown St, Darlinghurst; ☺4pm-midnight; 🚌333, 380, ▣Museum)

Eau-de-Vie COCKTAIL BAR

33 🚇 MAP P114, E2

Take the door marked 'restrooms' at the back of the main bar at the **Kirketon Hotel** (☎02-9332 2011; www.kirketon.com.au; 229 Darlinghurst Rd, Darlinghurst; r $149-389; ▣❄🛜; ▣Kings Cross) and enter this sophisticated, black-walled speak-easy, where a team of dedicated shirt-and-tie-wearing mixologists concoct the sort of beverages that win best-cocktail gongs. (☎0422 263 226; www.eaudevie.com.au; 229 Darlinghurst Rd, Darlinghurst; ☺6pm-1am Mon-Sat, to midnight Sun; 🛜; ▣Kings Cross)

Beresford Hotel PUB

34 🚇 MAP P114, D5

The well-polished tiles of the facade and interior are a real feature at this elegantly refurbished historic pub. It's a popular pre-club venue for an upmarket mixed crowd at weekends but makes for

Love, Tilly Devine (p123)

a quieter retreat midweek. The front bar is as handsome as they come; out the back is one of the area's best beer gardens, while upstairs is a schmick live-music and club space. (☑02-9114 7328; www.merivale.com.au/theberesfordhotel; 354 Bourke St, Surry Hills; ⏱noon-midnight Mon-Thu, to 1am Fri-Sun; �🛜; 🚌374, 397, 399)

Local Taphouse   PUB

35 🚇 MAP P114, E5

Beer lovers can test their palates against the tasting notes as they work their way through dozens of craft beers at this angular old pub. There are around 20 on tap, rotating regularly, so there's always something new to try. There aren't any views but the little high-sided rooftop is a great spot to catch

the breeze. (☑02-9360 0088; www.taphousedarlo.com.au; 122 Flinders St, Darlinghurst; ⏱noon-midnight Mon-Thu, to 1am Fri & Sat, to 11pm Sun; 🚌396-399)

Winery   WINE BAR

36 🚇 MAP P114, C4

Beautifully situated back from the road in the leafy grounds of a historic water reservoir, this oasis serves dozens of wines by the glass to the swankier Surry Hills set. Sit for a while and you'll notice all kinds of kitsch touches lurking in the greenery: headless statues, upside-down parrots, iron koalas. It's a very fun, boisterous scene on weekend afternoons. (☑02-8322 2007; www.thewinerysurryhills.com.au; 285a Crown St, Surry Hills; ⏱noon-midnight; 🛜; 🚇Central)

Palms on Oxford

GAY, CLUB

37 MAP P114, D3

No one admits to coming here, but the lengthy queues prove they are lying. In this underground dance bar, the heyday of Stock Aitken Waterman never ended. It may be uncool, but if you don't scream when Kylie hits the turntables, you'll be the only one. Lots of fun and a friendly place. Entry is usually free; no open-toed shoes allowed. (02-9357 4166; 124 Oxford St, Darlinghurst; 8pm-midnight Thu & Sun, to 3am Fri & Sat; 333, 380)

Stonewall Hotel

GAY, BAR

38 MAP P114, D3

Nicknamed 'Stonehenge' by those who think it's archaic, Stonewall, in a good-looking building, has three levels of bars and dance floors. Cabaret, karaoke and quiz nights spice things up; there's something on every night of the week. Wednesday's Malebox is an inventive way to bag yourself a boy. (02-9360 1963; www.stonewallhotel.com; 175 Oxford St, Darlinghurst; noon-4am; 333,380)

Arq

GAY, CLUB

39 MAP P114, D4

If Noah had to fill his Arq with groovy gay clubbers, he'd head here with a big net and some tranquillisers. This flash megaclub has a cocktail bar, a recovery room and two dance floors with high-energy house, drag shows and a hyperactive smoke machine. (02-9380 8700; www.arqsydney.com.au; 16 Flinders St, Darlinghurst; 9pm-3.30am Thu-Sun; 333, 380)

Belvoir St Theatre

Entertainment

Golden Age Cinema & Bar
CINEMA

40 ⭐ MAP P114, B3

In what was once the Sydney HQ of Paramount pictures, a heart-warming small cinema has taken over the former screening room downstairs. It shows old favourites, art-house classics and a few recherché gems. There's a great small bar here too, with free gigs on Thursdays and Saturdays. All up, it's a fabulous place for a night out. (☏02-9211 1556; www.ourgolden age.com.au; 80 Commonwealth St, Surry Hills; adult/concession tickets $21/17; ⏱4pm-midnight Tue-Fri, 2.30pm-midnight Sat, 2.30-11pm Sun; 🚊Museum)

Belvoir St Theatre
THEATRE

41 ⭐ MAP P114, B7

In a quiet corner of Surry Hills, this intimate venue, with two small stages, is the home of an often-experimental and consistently excellent theatre company that specialises in quality Australian drama. It often commissions new works and is a vital cog in the Sydney theatre scene. (☏02-9699 3444; www.belvoir.com.au; 25 Belvoir St, Surry Hills; 🚊372, 🚆Surry Hills, 🚆Central)

Venue 505
LIVE MUSIC

42 ⭐ MAP P114, A8

Focusing on jazz, roots, reggae, funk, gypsy and Latin music, this small, relaxed venue is artist-run and thoughtfully programmed. The space features comfortable couches and murals by a local painter. It does pasta, pizza and share plates so you can munch along to the music. (☏0419 294 755; www.venue505.com; 280 Cleveland St, Surry Hills; ⏱6pm-midnight Mon-Sat; 🚊372, 🚆Central)

Oxford Art Factory
LIVE MUSIC

43 ⭐ MAP P114, C2

Indie kids party against an arty backdrop at this two-room multipurpose venue modelled on Andy Warhol's NYC creative base. There's a gallery, a bar and a performance space that often hosts international acts and DJs. Check the website for what's on. (☏02-9332 3711; www.oxfordartfac tory.com; 38-46 Oxford St, Darlinghurst; 🚆Museum)

Shopping

Artery
ART

44 🅰 MAP P114, E2

Step into a world of mesmerising dots and swirls at this small gallery devoted to Aboriginal art. Artery's motto is 'ethical, contemporary, affordable', and while large canvases by established artists cost in the thousands, small, unstretched canvases start at around $35. There's also a good range of giftware as well as an offbeat sideline in preserved insects. (☏02-9380 8234; www.artery. com.au; 221 Darlinghurst Rd, Darlinghurst; ⏱10am-5pm; 🚆Kings Cross)

Ariel   BOOKS

45 🔒 MAP P114, D3

This well-loved bookstore has moved down the road from Paddington. It's an eclectic, savvy place that's particularly good on art and design and is also a fine spot to pick up an offbeat gift for someone. (📞02-9332 4581; www.arielbooks.com.au; 98 Oxford St, Darlinghurst; ⏰9.30am-7pm Mon-Wed, 9.30am-8pm Thu & Fri, 10am-8pm Sat, 11am-6pm Sun; 🚍333, 380)

Route 66   CLOTHING, VINTAGE

46 🔒 MAP P114, C3

The name says it all. This store has been around for decades, furnishing Sydney with new and pre-owned jeans, cowboy boots and other essential Americana. (📞02-9331 6686; www.route66.com.au; 255 Crown St, Darlinghurst; ⏰10.30am-6pm Mon-Wed, Fri & Sat, 10.30am-7.30pm Thu, noon-5pm Sun; 🚍330, 380, 🚆Museum)

Baby Likes to Pony   CLOTHING

47 🔒 MAP P114, E4

Stunning avant-garde lingerie, corsetry and accessories are on offer in this friendly store just off Oxford St where Darlinghurst blends into Paddington. (📞0488 766 966; www.babylikestopony.com; 319 South Dowling St, Darlinghurst; ⏰noon-6.30pm Mon-Wed, Fri & Sat, to 8pm Thu; 🚍333, 352, 380)

Makery   ARTS & CRAFTS

48 🔒 MAP P114, D3

This ample corner space is an innovative idea that lets local artisans and designers sell their products in a single space. There's an excellent range of everything from jewellery to candles to clothing; it's always worth a browse. (📞0410 471 144; www.work-shop.com.au; 106 Oxford St, Darlinghurst; ⏰10.30am-6.30pm Tue-Fri, 10am-5pm Sat, 11am-4pm Sun; 🚍333, 380)

Title   BOOKS, MUSIC

49 🔒 MAP P114, C7

Focusing on distinct pop-cultural streams, seemingly determined at random (but probably at the owner's whim – very *High Fidelity*), this offbeat little store is well-stocked with glossy hardbacks (everything from rock photography to cookbooks), cult DVDs and an eclectic range of music on vinyl and CD. It's a browser's paradise. (📞02-9699 7333; www.titlemusicfilmbooks.com; 499 Crown St, Surry Hills; ⏰10am-6pm Mon-Sat, 11am-5pm Sun; 🚆Surry Hills, 🚆Central)

Sax Fetish   ADULT

50 🔒 MAP P114, D3

No, it's not a bar for jazz obsessives, but rather a sexy, dark-hearted shop selling high-quality leather and rubber gear. All genders are catered for, and the 'accessories' range goes a little further than your standard belts and handbags (cufflinks and ties take on a whole new meaning here). (☏02-9331 6105; www.saxfetish.com; 110a Oxford St, Darlinghurst; ⏰noon-6pm Sun & Mon, 11am-7pm Tue, Wed & Fri, 11am-8pm Thu, 11am-6pm Sat; 🚌333, 380)

Robin Gibson Gallery ART

51 🔒 MAP P114, E2

Housed in a beautiful three-storey terrace behind a lush stand of palm trees, this long-established gallery represents a coterie of Australian artists, and also stages the occasional exhibition by international superstars. (☏02-9331 6692; www.robingibson.net; 278 Liverpool St, Darlinghurst; ⏰11am-6pm Tue-Sat; 🚃Kings Cross)

Bookshop Darlinghurst BOOKS

52 🔒 MAP P114, D4

This outstanding bookshop specialises in gay and lesbian tomes, with everything from queer crime and lesbian fiction to glossy pictorials and porn. A diverting browse, to say the least. (☏02-9331 1103; www.thebookshop.com.au; 207 Oxford St, Darlinghurst; ⏰10am-7pm Mon-Sat, noon-6pm Sun; 🚌333, 380)

FAIRFAX MEDIA VIA GETTY IMAGES ©

Route 66

Zoo Emporium VINTAGE

53 🔒 MAP P114, D4

One of several vintage shops near the intersection of Crown and Campbell Streets, this has two floors of gloriously loud '70s and '80s apparel. The ground floor is mostly discounted items, including a bargain bin. (☏02-9380 5990; 180 Campbell St, Darlinghurst; ⏰11am-6pm Mon-Wed, Fri & Sat, 11am-8pm Thu, noon-5pm Sun; 🚌333, 380)

Explore ⊚
Kings Cross & Potts Point

Traditionally Sydney's seedy red-light zone, the Cross has changed markedly in recent years. Lockout laws have killed the late-night bar life, and major building programs have accelerated gentrification in this so-close-to-the-city district. Adjoining the Cross, gracious, tree-lined Potts Point and Elizabeth Bay seem worlds away. Below by the water the old sailors' district of Woolloomooloo is a great spot for glitzy wharf restaurants and a handful of pubs of some character.

Kings Cross and its adjacent locales are ideal for exploring on foot; allocate half a day for the area to take in its quiet neighbourhood feel, but be sure to plan a revisit in the evening for the restaurant scene.

It makes sense to start around the Cross itself, at the top of William Street, and let gravity draw your wanders downwards.

Getting There & Around

🚇 Everywhere is within walking distance of Kings Cross train station.

🚌 Bus 311 hooks through Kings Cross, Potts Point, Elizabeth Bay and Woolloomooloo on its way from Railway Sq to the bottom of town. Buses 324 and 325 pass through Kings Cross (Bayswater Rd) en route between Walsh Bay, the City and Watsons Bay.

Kings Cross & Potts Point Map on p134

Kings Cross & Potts Point Map on p134

View over Woolloomooloo (p132) and Potts Point

Walking Tour 🥾

Wandering Around Woolloomooloo

Squeezed between the Domain and Kings Cross, Woolloomooloo (show us another word with eight Os!) is a suburb in transition. Once solidly working class, it still has some rough edges, but down by the water they're hard to spot. The navy base is still here, but drunken sailors are in short supply.

Walk Facts

Start Embarkation Park

Finish Old Fitzroy

Length 2.1km, 45 minutes

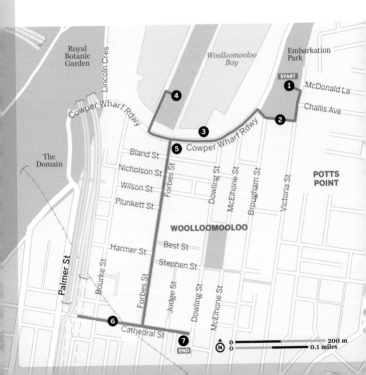

❶ Embarkation Park

This hidden **park** (Victoria St, Potts Point; ⧼Kings Cross) on the roof of a navy car park is a prime spot for surveying Woolloomooloo beneath your feet. There are usually a couple Royal Australian Navy ships moored at the Garden Island base below.

❷ Descend McElhone Stairs

These stone **stairs** (Victoria St, Potts Point; ⧼Kings Cross) were built in 1870 to connect spiffy Potts Point with the Woolloomooloo slums below. The steep steps run past an apartment block: residents sip tea on their balconies and stare bemusedly at the fitness freaks punishing themselves on the 113-stair uphill climb.

❸ Snack at Harry's Cafe de Wheels

Sure, it's a humble pie cart, but **Harry's** (Cowper Wharf Roadway, Woolloomooloo) is a tourist attraction nonetheless. Open since 1938 (except when founder Harry 'Tiger' Edwards was on active service), Harry's has served the good stuff to everyone from Pamela Anderson to Colonel Sanders.

❹ Woolloomooloo Wharf

A former wool and cargo dock, this beautiful Edwardian wharf (p135) faced oblivion for decades before a 2½-year demolition-workers' green ban on the site in the late 1980s saved it. It received a huge sprucing up in the late 1990s and has emerged as one of Sydney's most exclusive eating, drinking, sleeping and marina addresses.

❺ Space Out in Artspace

Artspace (p135) is spacey: its eternal quest is to fill the void with vigorous, engaging contemporary art. Things here are decidedly avant-garde – expect lots of conceptual pieces, audio visual installations and new-media masterpieces.

❻ Pace Cathedral Street

Cathedral Street, the heart of Woolloomooloo, glows purple with jacarandas in November. Walk along the street to get a feel for the suburb and how it is changing, with spiffy renovated terraces alongside social housing buildings.

❼ Settle in at the Old Fitzroy

Islington meets Melbourne in the back streets of Woolloomooloo: this totally unpretentious theatre pub (p139) is also a decent old-fashioned boozer in its own right.

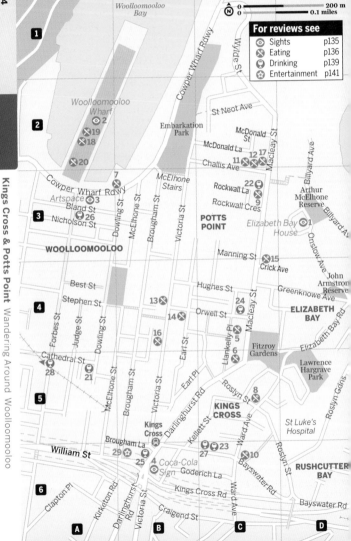

Woolloomooloo Bay

Cowper Wharf Rdwy

Wylde St

200 m
0.1 miles

For reviews see

	Sights	p135
	Eating	p136
	Drinking	p139
	Entertainment	p141

St Neot Ave

Woolloomooloo Wharf 2

McDonald St

Embarkation Park

McDonald St

McDonald La

19
18

Macleay St

11 12 17

Challis Ave

20

Cowper Wharf Rdwy

7

McElhone Stairs

Rockwall La 22

9

Billyard Ave

Arthur McElhone Reserve

Artspace 3

Bland St

Rockwall Cres

Billyard Av

Nicholson St

26

POTTS POINT

Elizabeth Bay House

Onslow Ave

Elizabeth Bay 1

WOOLLOOMOOLOO

Dowling St

McElhone St

Brougham St

Victoria St

Manning St 15

Crick Ave

John Armstrong Reserve

Greenknowe Ave

Best St

Hughes St

ELIZABETH BAY

Stephen St

13

24

Orwell St

Elizabeth Bay Rd

14

Forbes St

Judge St

Dowling St

McElhone St

16

Earl St

Llankelly Pl

5

6

Fitzroy Gardens

Lawrence Hargrave Park

Roslyn Gdns

Cathedral St

28

21

Brougham St

Victoria St

Earl Pl

Darlinghurst Rd

Roslyn St

8

KINGS CROSS

St Luke's Hospital

Kellett St

Ward Ave

29

Kings Cross

25 4 Coca-Cola Sign

27 23

Goderich La

10

Bayswater Rd

RUSHCUTTER BAY

William St

Brougham La

Darlinghurst Rd

Victoria St

Kings Cross Rd

Ward Ave

Roslyn St

Clapton Pl

Kirketon Rd

Darlinghurst Rd

Victoria St

Craigend St

Bayswater Rd

Sights

Elizabeth Bay House

HISTORIC BUILDING

1 ⊙ MAP P134, D3

Now dwarfed by 20th-century apartments, Colonial Secretary Alexander Macleay's elegant Greek Revival mansion was one of the finest houses in the colony when it was completed in 1839. The architectural highlight is an exquisite oval saloon with a curved and cantilevered staircase. There are lovely views over the harbour from the upstairs rooms. Drop down to the twin cellars for an introductory audiovisual with a weird beginning.

The grounds – a sort of botanical garden for Macleay, who collected plants from around the world – extended from the harbour all the way up the hill to Kings Cross. Traces remain, including a little **hidden grotto** reached by taking a path between 16 and 18 Onslow Ave. (☑02-9356 3022; www.sydneylivingmuseums.com.au; 7 Onslow Ave, Elizabeth Bay; adult/child $12/8; ⊙11am-4pm Fri-Sun; ☑311, ☒Kings Cross)

Woolloomooloo Wharf

HISTORIC BUILDING

2 ⊙ MAP P134, A2

A former wool and cargo dock, this beautiful Edwardian wharf faced oblivion for decades before a 2½-year demolition-workers' green ban on the site in the late 1980s saved it. It received a huge sprucing up in the late 1990s and has emerged as one of Sydney's most exclusive eating, sleeping and marina addresses.

It's still a public space, so feel free to explore the innards, past industrial conveyor-belt relics and a **hotel** (☑02-9331 9000; www.ovolohotels.com.au; 6 Cowper Wharf Rdwy; r $400-700; P ⊙ ❄ @ ☎ ☒). Along the way the wharf's history is etched into glass walls. You might even squeeze in some star-spotting – everyman-megastar Russell Crowe is one of several personalities to have a plush pad here. (Finger Wharf; Cowper Wharf Roadway, Woolloomooloo; ☑311, ☒Kings Cross)

Artspace

GALLERY

3 ⊙ MAP P134, A3

Artspace is spacey: its eternal quest is to fill the void with vigorous, engaging Australian and international contemporary art. Things here are decidedly avant-garde – expect lots of conceptual art, audio-visual installations and new-media pieces. It's an admirable attempt to liven things up in Sydney's art scene, experimenting with sometimes disturbing concepts. Disabled access is excellent. (☑02-9356 0555; www.artspace.org.au; 43-51 Cowper Wharf Rd, Woolloomooloo; admission free; ⊙11am-5pm Mon-Fri, to 6pm Sat & Sun; ☑311, ☒Kings Cross)

Coca-Cola Sign

LANDMARK

4 ⊙ MAP P134, B6

A Sydney landmark, this huge sign marks the entrance to Kings Cross. You're actually looking at the 2016 model: the previous one was replaced, then auctioned off letter by letter for local homeless charity the Wayside Chapel. (Darlinghurst Rd, Kings Cross; 🚇Kings Cross)

Eating

Room 10 CAFE $

5 ✖ MAP P134, C4

With a real neighbourhood feel, this tiny cafe is the sort of place where staff know all the locals by name. The coffee is delicious and the menu limited to sandwiches, salads and such – tasty and uncomplicated. Watch them make it in front of you as you sit at impossibly tiny tables or do some people-watching on this lovable laneway. (📞0432 445 342; www.facebook.com/room10espresso; 10 Llankelly Pl, Kings Cross; mains $8-14; ⏰7am-4pm Mon-Fri, 8am-4pm Sat & Sun; 🗡; 🚇Kings Cross)

What's in a Name?

Where exactly is Kings Cross? Although technically it's just the intersection of William and Victoria Sts, in reality it's more of a mindset than an exact geographical place. Much of what most people call Kings Cross falls within the suburb of Potts Point; businesses tend to use a Potts Point address if they want to sound classy and Kings Cross if they want to emphasise their party cred. Either way, you'll know Kings Cross when you see it.

Douce France CAFE $

6 ✖ MAP P134, C5

Locals love the croissants at this welcoming cafe on the main strip through the Cross. Other tempting patisserie options and pleasing coffee make this a top stop. Grab an outdoor table to watch the Cross characters parade past. (www.facebook.com/coffeefrench DouceFrance; 7 Darlinghurst Rd, Kings Cross; breakfasts $6-14; ⏰7am-7pm Mon-Fri, 8am-5.30pm Sat & Sun; 🛜; 🚌311, 🚇Kings Cross)

Harry's Cafe de Wheels FAST FOOD $

7 ✖ MAP P134, B3

Open since 1938 (except for a few years when founder Harry 'Tiger' Edwards was on active service), Harry's has been serving meat pies to everyone from Pamela Anderson to Frank Sinatra and Colonel Sanders. You can't leave without trying a 'Tiger': a hot meat pie with sloppy peas, mashed potato, gravy and tomato sauce. (📞02-9357 3074; www.harryscafedewheels.com.au; Cowper Wharf Roadway, Woolloomooloo; pies $5-8; ⏰8.30am-2am Mon & Tue, to 3am Wed & Thu, to 4am Fri, 9am-4am Sat, 9am-1am Sun; 🚌311, 🚇Kings Cross)

Piccolo Bar CAFE $

8 ✖ MAP P134, C5

A surviving slice of the old bohemian Cross, this tiny cafe hasn't changed much in over 60 years. The walls are covered in movie-star memorabilia, and new owners are faithful to the unique atmosphere created by locally legendary former owner Vittorio, who still drops by for a chat. (☎02-9368 1356; www.facebook.com/piccolobarcafe; 6 Roslyn St, Kings Cross; light meals $5-10; ☉6am-midnight Wed-Fri, 7am-midnight Sat & Sun; ☎; ☒Kings Cross)

Cho Cho San JAPANESE $$

9 🍴 MAP P134, C3

Glide through the shiny brass sliding door and take a seat at the communal table that runs the length of this stylish Japanese restaurant, all polished concrete and blond wood. The food is just as artful as the surrounds, with tasty izakaya-style bites emanating from both the raw bar and the hibachi grill. There's a good sake selection, too. (☎02-9331 6601; www.chochosan.com.au; 73 Macleay St, Potts Point; mains $22-38; ☉5.30-11pm Mon-Thu, noon-11pm Fri-Sun; ☒311, ☒Kings Cross)

Farmhouse MODERN AUSTRALIAN $$

10 🍴 MAP P134, C6

Occupying a space between restaurant and supper club, this narrow sliver of a place has a tiny kitchen and a charming host. Diners sit at one long table and eat a set menu that features uncomplicated, delicious dishes from high-quality produce. There are good wines and a buzzy, fun atmosphere. Prebooking is essential. (☎0448 413 791; www.farmhousekingscross.com.au; 4/40 Bayswater Rd, Kings Cross; set menu $60; ☉sittings 6.30pm & 8.30pm Wed-Sat, 2pm & 6.30pm Sun; ☒Kings Cross)

Fratelli Paradiso ITALIAN $$

11 🍴 MAP P134, C2

This underlit trattoria has them queuing at the door (especially on weekends). The intimate room showcases seasonal Italian dishes cooked with Mediterranean zing. Lots of busy black-clad waiters, lots of Italian chatter, lots of over-sized sunglasses. No bookings. (☎02-9357 1744; www.fratelliparadiso.com; 12-16 Challis Ave, Potts Point; breakfast $12-17, mains $25-39; ☉7am-11pm Mon-Sat, to 10pm Sun; ☒311, ☒Kings Cross)

Fish Shop SEAFOOD $$

12 🍴 MAP P134, C2

Decked out in bright Hamptons style, this brings a coastal breeze to Challis Ave with casual but high-quality fish dishes served all day, and some nice wines to accompany them. It's also great for a quick snack – some oysters or a fish burger – and a glass of something. (☎02-9114 7340; www.merivale.com.au/thefishshop; 22 Challis Ave, Potts Point; mains $28-38; ☉noon-10pm Mon-Fri, to 11pm Sat, to 9pm Sun; ☒311, ☒Kings Cross)

Butler LATIN AMERICAN $$

13 🍴 MAP P134, B4

There's a real wow factor to the verdant back terrace of this Potts Point bar-restaurant, with its spectacular city skyline views. The breezy vibe and furniture make it a prime spot to get stuck into share plates that take influences from across the Caribbean and Latin America. (☏02-8354 0742; www.butlersydney.com.au; 123 Victoria St, Potts Point; large share plates $30-36; ⏰4-11pm Mon, noon-midnight Tue-Sat, noon-10pm Sun; 🛜; 🚉Kings Cross)

Chester White   ITALIAN $$

14 ☒ MAP P134, B4

Calling itself a 'cured diner', this diminutive corner eatery, named after a breed of pig, serves nine different kinds of cured meats, a large variety of pickled vegetables and a few simple mains (pasta and the like). Grab a chrome stool by the kitchen/bar, sip on an Italian wine and watch the hipster lads slicing and dicing away. (☏02-9332 3692; www.chesterwhitediner.com.au; 3 Orwell St, Kings Cross; dishes $14-23;

Old Fitzroy Hotel

⏰5-11pm Tue-Thu, noon-11pm Fri & Sat; 🚉Kings Cross)

Apollo   GREEK $$

15 ☒ MAP P134, C4

An excellent exemplar of modern Greek cooking, this taverna has stylish and fashionable decor, a well-priced menu of share plates and a bustling vibe. Starters are particularly impressive, especially the pitta bread hot from the oven, the fried saganaki cheese with honey and oregano, and the wild-weed and cheese pie. (☏02-8354 0888; www.theapollo.com.au; 44 Macleay St, Elizabeth Bay; mains $26-38; ⏰6-11pm Mon-Thu, noon-11pm Fri & Sat, noon-9.30pm Sun; 🚌311, 🚉Kings Cross)

Ms G's   ASIAN $$

16 ☒ MAP P134, B4

Offering a cheeky, irreverent take on Asian cooking (hence the name – geddit?), Ms G's is nothing if not an experience. It can be loud, frantic and painfully hip, but the adventur-ous combinations of pan-Asian and European flavours have certainly got some spark. (☏02-9114 7342; www.merivale.com/msgs; 155 Victoria St, Potts Point; mains $22-36; ⏰6-11pm Mon-Thu, noon-3pm & 6-11pm Fri & Sat, 1-9pm Sun; 🛜; 🚉Kings Cross)

Yellow   VEGETARIAN $$$

17 ☒ MAP P134, C2

This sunflower-yellow former art-ists' residence is now a top-notch contemporary vegetarian restaurant. Dishes are prepared with real panache, and excellent flavour combinations are present throughout. The tasting menus, which can be vegan, take the Sydney meat-free scene to new levels and the service is not too formal. Weekend brunch is also a highlight, as is the wine list. (☑02-9332 2344; www.yellowsydney. com.au; 57 Macleay St, Potts Point; 5-/7-course degustation menu $75/95; ☉6-11pm Mon-Fri, 11am-3pm & 6-11pm Sat & Sun; ☝; ☐311, ☐Kings Cross)

China Doll   ASIAN $$$

18 ❌ MAP P134, A2

Gaze over the Woolloomooloo marina and city skyline as you tuck into deliciously inventive dishes drawing inspiration from all over Asia. The setting on the finger wharf is memorable, but the food keeps up, with delicious textures and flavour combinations. Plates are designed to be shared; there are also a few dim-sum-style options. (☑02-9380 6744; www.chinadoll.com. au; 4/6 Cowper Wharf Roadway, Woolloomooloo; mains $36-46; ☉noon-3pm & 6-10.30pm; ☐311, ☐Kings Cross)

Otto Ristorante   ITALIAN $$$

19 ❌ MAP P134, A2

Forget the glamorous waterfront location and the A-list crowd – Otto will be remembered for single-handedly dragging Sydney's Italian cooking into the new century with dishes such as artisan *strozzapreti* pasta with fresh Yamba prawns, tomato, chilli and black olives. Its opening hours

mean you can often grab a table here on spec mid-afternoon, but booking at meal times is essential. (☑02-9368 7488; www.ottoristorante. com.au; 8/6 Cowper Wharf Rdwy, Woolloomooloo; mains $43-56; ☉noon-10pm; ☐311, ☐Kings Cross)

Aki's   INDIAN $$$

20 ❌ MAP P134, A2

The first cab off the rank as you walk onto Woolloomooloo's wharf is Aki's. This is beautifully presented, intuitively constructed high-Indian cuisine, supplemented by a six-page wine list showcasing local and international drops. And the setting, of course, is just marvellous. (☑02-9332 4600; www.akisindian. com.au; 1/6 Cowper Wharf Roadway, Woolloomooloo; mains $32-34; ☉noon-3pm & 6-10.30pm Sun-Fri, 6-10.30pm Sat; ☝; ☐311, ☐Kings Cross)

Drinking

Old Fitzroy Hotel   PUB

21 🍺 MAP P134, A5

A gem hidden in the backstreets of Woolloomooloo, this totally unpretentious theatre (p141) is also a decent old-fashioned boozer in its own right, with a great variety of beers on tap and a convivial welcome. Prop up the bar, grab a seat at a streetside table or head upstairs to the bistro, pool table and couches. (☑02-9356 3848; www.oldfitzroy.com.au; 129 Dowling St, Woolloomooloo; ☉11am-midnight Mon-Fri, noon-midnight Sat, 3-10pm Sun; ☞; ☐Kings Cross)

Party's Over

Formerly Sydney's premier party precinct, this neighbourhood has had much of the life sucked out of it by the central Sydney licensing laws introduced in 2014. Most of the late-night clubs have closed, though a couple are still going. On the upside, the streets look less like a war zone in the wee hours.

Monopole   WINE BAR

22 🚇 MAP P134, C3

Dark and sexy, Monopole seduces with its stylish interior, complete with hanging strips of black sound-absorption material and discreet front screen. A fabulous wine list of Australian and international producers offers over 20 vintages by the glass or carafe, so an impromptu tasting session is easy. The food is great too, with house-cured charcuterie and intriguing cheeses a highlight. (📞02-9360 4410; www.monopolesydney.com.au; 71a Macleay St, Potts Point; ⏱5pm-midnight Mon-Fri, noon-midnight Sat, noon-10pm Sun; 📶; 🚌311, 🚉Kings Cross)

World Bar   BAR, CLUB

23 🚇 MAP P134, C6

A reformed bordello is an unpretentious, grungy club with three floors to lure in backpackers and cheap drinks to loosen things up. DJs play indie, hiphop, power pop and house nightly. Wednesday (The Wall) and Saturday are the big nights. In the earlier evening, it's a pleasant place for a quiet drink on the foliage-rich verandah. There's a theatre, too. (📞02-9357 7700; www.theworldbar.com; 24 Bayswater Rd, Kings Cross; ⏱2pm-midnight Sun & Mon, to 3.30am Tue-Sat; 📶; 🚉Kings Cross)

Roosevelt   COCKTAIL BAR

24 🚇 MAP P134, C4

The low-lit seductive glamour of this sleek and stylish cocktail bar takes you right back to the '20s, though it's named for a local postwar gangster's haunt. They take their cocktails seriously here, making them in front of you with great panache – and they are seriously good. (📞0423 203 119; www.theroosevelt.com.au; 32 Orwell St, Kings Cross; ⏱5pm-midnight Mon-Fri, noon-midnight Sat, 3-10pm Sun; 📶; 🚌311, 🚉Kings Cross)

Kings Cross Hotel   PUB

25 🚇 MAP P134, B6

This grand old brick building guards the entrance to the Cross and is one of the area's best pubs, with several levels of boozy entertainment. The balcony bar is a very pleasant spot for lunch, while the rooftop that opens weekend evenings has the drawcard vistas. Saturdays are good, with DJs on all levels. (📞02-9331 9900; www.kingscrosshotel.com.au; 244-248 William St, Kings Cross; ⏱10am-1am Mon-Thu, to 3.30am Fri & Sat, to midnight Sun; 📶; 🚉Kings Cross)

Tilbury PUB

26 MAP P134, A3

Once the dank domain of burly sailors and salty ne'er-do-wells, the Tilbury now sparkles. An upmarket crowd of Potts Pointers and yachties populate the light, bright interiors, sipping G&Ts and glasses of imported wine. The restaurant does top-notch contemporary fare; the seats out the front, in the upstairs bar and in the gin garden are particularly popular on lazy Sunday afternoons. (02-9368 1955; www.tilburyhotel.com.au; 12-18 Nicholson St, Woolloomooloo; 11am-10pm Mon-Wed, 11am-midnight Thu & Fri, 10am-midnight Sat, 10am-10pm Sun; 311, Kings Cross)

Candy's Apartment CLUB

27 MAP P134, C6

It's dark and very sweaty in this subterranean venue with two bars, a dance floor with DJs spinning house and other electronica, and a space for bands to play. They pack 'em in and you'll find plenty of guys and gals scanning the crowd hoping they won't go home alone. (02-9380 5600; www.candys.com.au; 22 Bayswater Rd, Kings Cross; 8pm-4am Fri & Sat; Kings Cross)

East Sydney Hotel PUB

28 MAP P134, A5

Not a poker machine is in sight at this beautiful traditional corner boozer in a quiet area of Woolloomooloo. Open since 1856, it's a place of great character, perfect for sipping a quiet schooner of beer while reading the paper. Uncomplicated pub grub is also available. (02-9358 1975; www.eastsydneyhotel.com; cnr Crown & Cathedral Sts, Woolloomooloo; 11.30am-midnight Sun-Tue, to 1am Wed & Thu, to 3am Fri & Sat; 311, St James)

Entertainment

Old Fitz Theatre THEATRE

Is it a pub? A theatre? A bistro? Actually, it's all three. Grassroots company Red Line Productions stages loads of new Australian plays at this likeable venue (see 21 Map p134, A5) in a quiet Woolloomooloo street. (0416 044 413; www.redlineproductions.com.au; 129 Dowling St, Woolloomooloo; $25-48; Kings Cross)

Happy Endings Comedy Club COMEDY

29 MAP P134, B6

Between 1955 and 1969 this was the city's premier finger-snappin', beret-wearing boho cellar bar, hosting performances by Frank Sinatra and Sarah Vaughan. Those heady days are long gone but good-quality stand-up comedy keeps this intimate venue buzzing. Book ahead for discounted admission. (El Rocco Room; 02-9130 5150; www.happyendingscomedyclub.com.au; 154 Brougham St, Potts Point; $27.50; shows 8.30pm Fri & Sat; Kings Cross)

Explore

Bondi to Coogee

Sydney sheds its suit and tie, ditches the strappy heels and chills out in the eastern suburbs. Beach after golden-sand beach, alternating with sheer sandstone cliffs, are the classic vistas of this beautiful, laid-back and egalitarian stretch of the city.

Improbably good-looking arcs of sand framed by jagged cliffs, the eastern beaches are a big part of the Sydney experience. Most famous of all is the broad sweep of Bondi Beach, where Sydney comes to see and be seen. South of Bondi, Bronte is a steep-sided beach 'burb, its bowl-shaped park strewn with picnic tables and barbecues. Further south is the concrete-fringed, safe-swimming inlet of Clovelly: a great place to dust off your snorkel. Next stop, heading south, is Coogee, with a wide, handsome beach and lively backpacker and local scene in the pubs and shops.

Getting There & Away

🚆 The Eastern Suburbs train line heads to Bondi Junction, which is 2.5km from Bondi Beach, 3km from Bronte Beach and 4km from Coogee Beach.

🚌 For Bondi, take bus 333 (express) or 380 from Circular Quay via Oxford St. For Coogee, take bus M50, 373 or 372 among others. It's quicker to get a bus from Bondi Junction station.

Bondi to Coogee Map on p148

Icebergs Pool (p145), Bondi Beach KOMPASSKIND.DE/SHUTTERSTOCK ©

Top Sight 📷
Bondi Beach

Definitively Sydney, Bondi is one of the world's great beaches: ocean and land collide, the Pacific arrives in great foaming swells and all people are equal, as democratic as sand. It's the closest ocean beach to the city centre (8km away), has consistently good (though crowded) waves, and is great for a rough-and-tumble swim.

◎ **MAP P148, E2**

Campbell Pde, Bondi

🚌 333, 380-2

Surf's Up

Two surf clubs patrol the beach between sets of red-and-yellow flags, positioned to avoid the worst rips and holes. Thousands of unfortunates have to be rescued from the surf each year, so don't become a statistic – swim between the flags. Surfers carve up sandbar breaks at either end of the beach; it's a good place for learners too.

Icebergs Pool

This famous saltwater **pool** (☎ 02-9130 4804; www.icebergs.com.au; 1 Notts Ave; adult/child $7/5; ⏱ 6am-6.30pm Mon-Wed & Fri, from 6.30am Sat & Sun), regularly doused by the breakers, commands the best view in Bondi and has a cute cafe (p153). There's a more sheltered pool for kids. It closes on Thursdays so they can clean the seaweed out.

The Pavilion

Built in a blended Mediterranean/Georgian Revival style in 1929, 'The Pav' is more a cultural centre than a changing shed, although it does have changing rooms, showers and lockers (small/large $4/6). There's a free art gallery upstairs, a theatre out the back, and various cafes and a bar lining the ocean frontage, including the extremely popular Bucket List (p156). Redevelopment plans had been put on hold at time of research.

Other Features

In summer there's an outdoor cinema (p157) behind the beach while at the southern end is a skate park. There's an outdoor workout area at the northern end, plus a park with barbecues. Alcohol is banned throughout.

★ Top Tips

o Swim between the red-and-yellow flags, which indicate areas patrolled by lifeguards.

o If the sea's angry or you have small children in tow, try the saltwater sea baths at either end of the beach.

o Surfers carve up sandbar breaks at either end of the beach; there's a **skate ramp** (Queen Elizabeth Dr; 🚌 333, 380-2) at the beach's southern tip.

o At the beach's northern end there's a grassy spot with coin-operated barbecues. Note that booze is banned on the beach.

✕ Take a Break

Once you've had your fill of the surf, head to the North Bondi RSL (p156) at the northern end of the beach.

Or at the trendier southern end, hit the Crabbe Hole cafe (p153) by the Icebergs pool.

Walking Tour 🚶

Bondi to Coogee

Arguably Sydney's most famous, most popular and best walk, this coastal path shouldn't be missed. Both ends are well connected to bus routes, as are most points in between should you feel too hot and bothered to continue – although a cooling dip at any of the beaches en route should cure that (pack your swimmers). There's little shade on this track, so make sure you dive into a tub of sunscreen before setting out.

Walk Facts

Start Bondi Beach
End Coogee Beach
Length 6km; three hours

❶ Bondi Beach

Starting at iconic Bondi Beach (p144), take the stairs up the south end to Notts Ave, passing above the glistening Icebergs pool complex. Step onto the clifftop trail at the end of Notts Ave. Walking south, the windswept sandstone cliffs and boisterous Pacific Ocean couldn't be more spectacular (watch for dolphins, whales and surfers).

❷ Tamarama Beach

Small but perfectly formed Tamarama (p150) has a deep reach of sand that is totally disproportionate to its width.

❸ Bronte Beach

Descend from the cliff tops onto Bronte Beach (p150). Take a dip, lay out a picnic under the Norfolk Island pines or head to a cafe for a caffeine hit. After your break, pick up the path on the southern side of the beach.

❹ Waverley Cemetery

Some famous Australians are among the subterranean denizens of the amazing cliff-edge Waverley Cemetery (p150). On a clear winter's day this is a prime vantage point for whale-watchers.

❺ Clovelly Beach

Pass the locals enjoying a beer or a game of lawn bowls at the Clovelly Bowling Club, then breeze past the cockatoos and canoodling lovers in Burrows Park to sheltered Clovelly Beach (p150).

❻ Gordons Bay

Follow the footpath up through the car park, along Cliffbrook Pde, then down the steps to the upturned dinghies lining Gordons Bay, one of Sydney's best shore-dive spots.

❼ Dolphin Point

The trail continues past **Dolphin Point** (Baden St, Coogee; 🚌313-14, 353, 370-4), which offers great ocean views and the Giles Baths ocean pool (p151). A sobering shrine commemorates the 2002 Bali bombings that killed many locals. The park's name was changed to honour the six members of the Coogee Dolphins rugby league team who died in the blast.

❽ Coogee Beach

The trail then lands you smack-bang on glorious Coogee Beach (p150). Swagger into the Coogee Bay Hotel (p156) and toast your efforts with a cold beverage.

Bondi Golf Club

Ben Buckler Point

Bay St

Military Rd

Wallis Pde

Hastings Pde

Brighton Blvd

Ramsgate Ave

Wairoa Ave

Bondi Bay

Bondi Beach

Campbell Pde

Blair St

Warners Ave

Beach Rd

Gould St

Curlewis St

Hall St

Lamrock Ave

Roscoe St

Gould St

Glenayr Ave

O'Brien St

Wellington St

Hall St

BONDI BEACH

Francis St

Edward St

Hunter Park

Hunter St

Wilga St

Marks Park

Mackenzies Bay

Glenayr Ave

Tamarama Beach

Tamarama Bay

TAMARAMA

Bondi Rd

Glen St

Dudley St

BONDI

Tamarama Park

Alfred St

Bronte Beach

Hewlett St

Bayview St

Bronte Park

Bronte Rd

Gardyne St

BRONTE

Old South Head Rd

Birriga Rd

Bellevue Park

Edgecliff Rd

Bellevue Rd

Cooper Park

Bondi Rd

Paul St

Martins Ave

Wellington St

Ocean St N

Penkivil St

Anglesea St

Park Pde

Avoca St

Watson St

King St

Stephen St

Ewell St

Birrell St

Belgrave St

Read St

Palmerston Ave

Murray St

Gipps St

WAVERLEY

Henrietta St

Wiley St

Waverley Park

BONDI JUNCTION

Syd Einfeld Dr

Council St

Paul St

Bondi Rd

Birrell St

Bronte Rd

WAVERLEY

Queens Park

Carrington Rd

Darley Rd

For reviews see

◉ Top Sights p144
⊙ Sights p150
⊗ Eating p152
⊗ Drinking p155
✪ Entertainment p157
⊞ Shopping p157

500 m
0.25 miles

Sights

Tamarama Beach BEACH

1 ◉ MAP P148, D4

Surrounded by high cliffs, Tamarama has a deep tongue of sand with just 80m of shoreline. Diminutive, yes, but ever-present rips make Tamarama the most dangerous patrolled beach in New South Wales; it's often closed to swimmers. Make sure you pay attention to the lifesavers. It's hard to picture now, but between 1887 and 1911 a rollercoaster looped out over the water as part of an amusement park. (Pacific Ave, Tamarama; 🚌 361)

Bronte Beach BEACH

2 ◉ MAP P148, C4

A winning family-oriented beach hemmed in by sandstone cliffs and a grassy park, Bronte lays claims to the title of the oldest surf lifesaving club in the world (1903). Contrary to popular belief, the beach is named after Lord Nelson, who doubled as the Duke of Bronte (a place in Sicily), and not the famous literary sorority. There's a kiosk and a changing room attached to the surf club, and covered picnic tables near the public barbecues. (Bronte Rd, Bronte; 🚼; 🚌 379)

Waverley Cemetery CEMETERY

3 ◉ MAP P148, C5

Many Sydneysiders would die for these views...and that's the only way they're going to get them. Blanketing the clifftops between Bronte and Clovelly beaches, the white marble gravestones here are dazzling in the sunlight. Eighty thousand people have been interred here since 1877, including writers Henry Lawson and Dorothea Mackellar, and cricketer Victor Trumper. It's an engrossing (and surprisingly uncreepy) place to explore, and maybe to spot a whale offshore during winter. The Bondi to Coogee coastal walk (p146) heads past it. (📞 02-9083 8899; www.waverleycemetery.com; St Thomas St, Bronte; 🕑 7am-5pm May-Sep, to 7pm Oct-Apr; 🚌 360, 379)

Clovelly Beach BEACH

4 ◉ MAP P148, C6

It might seem odd, but this concrete-edged ocean channel is a great place to swim, sunbathe and snorkel. It's safe for the kids, and despite the swell surging into the inlet, underwater visibility is great. Bring your goggles, but don't go killing anything...a beloved friendly grouper fish lived here for many years until he was speared by a tourist. (Clovelly Rd, Clovelly; 🚌 338-9)

Coogee Beach BEACH

5 ◉ MAP P148, B8

Bondi without the glitz and the posers, Coogee (locals pronounce the 'oo' as in the word 'took') has a deep sweep of sand, historic ocean baths and plenty of green space for barbecues and Frisbee hurling. There are lockers and showers here. Between the world wars, Coogee had an English-style pier, with a 1400-seat theatre and a 600-seat ballroom...until the surf took it.

At Coogee Beach's northern end, below Dolphin Point, **Giles Baths** is what's known as a 'bogey hole' – a semiformal rock pool open to the surging surf. At the beach's southern end, **Ross Jones Memorial Pool** has sandcastle-like concrete turrets. Both have free admission.

A short walk beyond the beach are the sea pools known as **McIver's** (Beach St; $2; ☺ sunrise-sunset; ☐ 352, 372-7) and **Wylie's** (☎ 02-9665 2838; www.wylies.com.au; 4b Neptune St; adult/child $5/2.50;

☺ 7am-7pm Oct-Mar, to 5pm Apr-Sep; ☐ 353, 376-7)

Offshore, compromising the surf here a little, is craggy Wedding Cake Island, immortalised in a surf-guitar instrumental by Midnight Oil. (Arden St, Coogee; www.randwick.nsw.gov.au; ☐ 313-14, 353, 370-4)

Mahon Pool SWIMMING

6 ◎ MAP P148, B8

Hidden within the cliffs, 500m north of Maroubra Beach, Mahon Pool is an idyllic rock pool where the surf crashes over the edges at high tide. It's quite possibly Sydney's most beautiful bogey hole (sea bath). (www.randwick.nsw.gov.au; Marine Pde, Maroubra; admission free; ☐ 353, 376-77)

Beach Culture

In the mid-1990s an enthusiastic businesswoman obtained a concession to rent loungers on Tamarama Beach and offer waiter service. Needless to say, it didn't last long. Even at what was considered at the time to be Sydney's most glamorous beach, nobody was interested in that kind of malarkey.

For Australians, going to the beach is all about rolling out a towel on the sand with a minimum of fuss. And they're certainly not prepared to pay for the privilege. Sandy-toed ice-cream vendors are acceptable; martini luggers are not. In summer one of the more unusual sights is the little coffee and ice-cream boat pulling up to Lady Bay (and other harbour beaches) and a polite queue of nude gentlemen forming to purchase their icy poles.

Surf lifesavers have a hallowed place in the culture and you'd do well to heed their instructions, not least of all because they're likely to be in your best interest. They're an Australian institution.

Eating

Lox Stock & Barrel JEWISH, CAFE $$

7 MAP P148, D1

Stare down the barrel of a smoking hot bagel and ask yourself one question: Wagyu corned-beef Reuben, or homemade pastrami and Russian coleslaw? In the evening the menu sets its sights on steak, lamb shoulder and slow-roasted eggplant. It's always busy, even on a wet Monday. (02-9300 0368; www. loxstockandbarrel.com.au; 140 Glenayr Ave, Bondi Beach; breakfast & lunch dishes $10-22, dinner $18-29; 7am-3.30pm daily plus 6-10pm Wed & Thu, to 11pm Fri & Sat; 379)

Earth to Table VEGAN, CAFE $

8 MAP P148, A3

Perfect if you follow a vegan, paleo or gluten-free diet, this place is hippy outside but hip inside. All the food is sugar-free, vegan and raw, and it's delicious. Smoothie bowls, cold-pressed coffee, organic teas, buckwheat pancakes: it's amazing what it manages to create. Chatty staff and ambient electronica make for a welcoming atmosphere. (02-9029 1755; www.earth totable.com.au; 85 Bronte Rd, Bondi Junction; mains $16-20; 8am-5pm Wed-Sun; Bondi Junction)

Funky Pies VEGAN, BAKERY $

9 MAP P148, D1

Taking the meat out of a meat pie would be considered un-Australian in some quarters but this tiny place does a great job of it. Really tasty vegan combinations can be accompanied by huge smoothies; grab one of the two outdoor tables or take away to the beach. The place has a social conscience too, supporting several charities. (0451 944 404; www.funkypies.com. au; 144 Glenayr Ave, Bondi Beach; pies $6.50; 8.30am-8.30pm Mon-Fri, from 10am Sat & Sun; 379)

Bonditony's Burger Joint BURGERS $

The squelch comes oozing out as you bite down on one of these sinfully tasty burgers from a rock 'n' roll–themed spot (see 9 Map p148, D1) a couple of blocks back from the beach. Prepare to wait a long time at weekends, as it's so popular. It's got a drinks licence though, so you can kick back with a beer while you do. (0410 893 003; www.bonditonysburgerjoint.com; 144 Glenayr Ave, Bondi Beach; burgers $15-17; noon-10pm Mon-Fri, 11am-10pm Sat, 11am-9pm Sun; 379)

La Piadina ITALIAN $

10 MAP P148, D1

A piadina is a filled flat bread common in northern Italy, and the Zizioli brothers are the only ones serving them in Sydney. Fillings include prosciutto, rocket, mozzarella and nduja, a spicy, spreadable Italian sausage. Have them for breakfast, lunch or dinner, but whatever you do, have them – they're delicious! (02-9300 0160; www.lapiadina.com.au;

106 Glenayr Ave, Bondi Beach; mains $13-18; ⏱8am-5pm Mon, to 10pm Tue-Sun; 🚌379)

Crabbe Hole
CAFE $

Tucked within the Icebergs pool complex (there's no need to pay admission if you're only eating), this crab-sized nook (see 18 ❌ Map p148, D3) is the kind of place locals would prefer we didn't let you know about. Toasted sandwiches, muesli, and banana bread star on the small but perfectly formed menu; coffees are automatic double shots unless you specify otherwise. The views are blissful. (📞0450 272 223; www.facebook.com/thecrabbehole; Lower Level, 1 Notts Ave, Bondi Beach; breakfasts $8-15; ⏱7am-3pm Mon-Fri, to 5pm Sat & Sun; 🚌333, 380-2)

Three Blue Ducks
CAFE $$

11 ❌ MAP P148, C5

These ducks are a fair waddle from the water at Bronte Beach, but that doesn't stop queues forming outside the graffiti-covered walls for weekend breakfasts across two seating areas. The adventurous chefs have a strong commitment to using local, organic and fair trade food whenever possible. It's part of a nice little eating strip. (📞02-9389 0010; www.threeblueducks.com; 141-143 Macpherson St, Bronte; breakfasts $14-22, lunches $20-32, dinners $28-38; ⏱6.30am-2.30pm daily plus 6-11pm Wed-Sat; 📶🅿; 🚌379)

Trio
CAFE $$

12 ❌ MAP P148, D2

Brunch in Bondi has become de rigueur in Sydney in recent years, and this friendly, unpretentious cafe is one of the top spots to do it. The menu covers several global influences, from Mexican chilaquiles to Middle Eastern shakshouka via some Italian bruschetta. It's a great way to start a day by the sea. (📞02-9365 6044; www.triocafe.com.au; 56 Campbell Pde, Bondi Beach; dishes $18-27; ⏱7am-3pm Mon-Fri, 7.30am-3.30pm Sat & Sun; 📶🅿; 🚌333, 380-2)

Bondi's Best
SEAFOOD $$

13 ❌ MAP P148, F1

In an appealing block of cafes close to the beach action but more peaceful, this little square place has more kitchen than customer space, but it's worth finding a spot for all-day fish 'n' chips as well as more elaborate fish and seafood, plus mealtime sushi and sashimi choices. It's all casual and tasty; there's a more restaurant-y outlet on Hall St in Bondi too. (📞02-9300 9886; www.bondisbest.com.au; 39-53 Campbell Pde, North Bondi; meals $15-30; ⏱noon-9pm; 🚻; 🚌333, 379, 380-2)

Cafe de France
FRENCH, CAFE $$

14 ❌ MAP P148, A8

An art nouveau building, posters of Paris, crêpes, croissants and croques monsieur...this friendly cafe is as French as South Coogee can get. There are breakfasts all day, as well as salads and classics such as steak frites for lunch. Dinners are memorable, with blackboard bistro specials like coq au vin. (📞02-9664 4005; www.cafedefrancecoogee.com.au; 19 Havelock Ave, Coogee; breakfast $11-17, dinner mains $29-36; 🕐7am-3.30pm Mon-Wed, 7am-3.30pm & 6-10pm Thu & Fri, 7.30am-10pm Sat, 7.30am-5pm Sun; 🚌353, 376-7)

Little Kitchen
CAFE $$

15 MAP P148, B8

Confident modern Australian fare, strong on presentation, vibrant flavours and quality ingredients, is on offer in this tiny spot. A cheerful, family-run business with an open kitchen and some outdoor seating, it fits well with Coogee's likeably casual beach vibe. Pre-beach breakfasts are a great option here too. (📞02-8021 3424; www.thelittle

Beach Eats 🍴

There are plentiful eating options in the beach suburbs, though heading away from the beachfront strip is often a good idea. Bondi has the biggest range of options, from brunchy cafes to upmarket restaurants. Coogee is another likely spot, while Bronte has a decent eating strip on Macpherson St, west of St Thomas St, which is a 10-minute walk back from the sand.

kitchen.com.au; 275 Arden St, Coogee; lunch mains $19-26, dinner mains $25-31; 🕐7am-3pm daily plus 6-9pm Thu, 6-10pm Fri & Sat; 🚌353, 376-7)

A Tavola
ITALIAN $$

16 MAP P148, D1

Carrying on the tradition of its Darlinghurst **sister** (📞02-9331 7871; 348 Victoria St, Darlinghurst; mains $22-35; 🕐noon-3pm & 6-11pm Mon-Sat; 🚆Kings Cross), Bondi's A Tavola gathers around a big communal marble table where, before the doors open, the pasta-making action happens. Expect robust flavours, impeccably groomed waiters and delicious homemade pasta. There's some pleasant outdoor seating on this interesting street. (📞02-9130 1246; www.atavola.com.au; 75 Hall St, Bondi Beach; mains $25-37; 🕐5.30-11pm Mon & Tue, noon-3pm & 5.30-11pm Wed-Sun; 📶; 🚌379)

Bondi Trattoria
ITALIAN $$

17 MAP P148, D2

For an all-day Bondi option with vistas, you can't go past the trusty 'Trat', as it's known in these parts. Tables spill out onto Campbell Pde for those hungry for beach views. New owners have given the menu a facelift, with quality antipasto options and excellent salads as well as pizzas, pasta and daily fish specials. (📞02-9365 4303; www.bonditrattoria.com.au; 34 Campbell Pde, Bondi Beach; breakfast $11-20, lunch & dinner $28-37; 🕐8am-10pm; 🅿; 🚌333, 380-2)

Icebergs Dining Room
ITALIAN $$$

18 MAP P148, D3

Poised above the famous Icebergs swimming pool (p145), Icebergs' views sweep across the Bondi Beach arc to the sea. Inside, bow-tied waiters deliver fresh, sustainably sourced seafood and steaks cooked with elan. There's also an elegant cocktail bar. In the same building, the Icebergs club has a bistro and bar with simpler, cheaper fare. (02-9365 9000; www.idrb.com; 1 Notts Ave, Bondi Beach; mains $46-52; noon-3pm & 6.30-11pm, from 10am Sun; 333, 380-2)

Sean's Panaroma
MODERN AUSTRALIAN $$$

19 MAP P148, E1

Sean Moran's ever-changing menu is chalked on a blackboard in this modest little dining room that packs out with happy diners. Ocean views, hearty seasonal dishes and friendly service make it a deservedly popular, buzzy spot. (02-9365 4924; www.seanspanarama.co; 270 Campbell Pde, Bondi Beach; mains $39-45; 6-10pm Wed-Sat, noon-4pm Sat & Sun; 333, 380-2)

Drinking

Coogee Pavilion
BAR

20 MAP P148, B7

With numerous indoor and outdoor bars, a kids' play area and a glorious adults-only rooftop, this vast complex has brought a touch of inner-city glam to Coogee. Built in 1887, the building originally housed an aquarium and swimming pools. Now, space, light and white wood give a breezy feel. Great eating options run from Mediterranean-inspired bar food to fish 'n' chips and sashimi.

It gets totally packed at weekends. (02-9114 7321; www.merivale.com.au/coogeepavilion; 169 Dolphin St, Coogee; 7.30am-midnight; ; 313-14, 353, 370-4)

Anchor
BAR

21 MAP P148, D2

Surfers, backpackers and the local cool kids slurp down icy margaritas at this bustling bar at the south end of the Bondi strip. It sports a dark-wood nautical-piratey feel and is also a great spot for a late snack. The two-hour happy hour from 5pm weekdays is a good way to start the post-surf debrief. (02-8084 3145; www.facebook.com/anchorbarbondi; 8 Campbell Pde, Bondi Beach; 5pm-midnight Mon-Fri, from noon Sat & Sun; ; 333, 380-382)

Neighbourhood
BAR

22 MAP P148, D1

This smart food and wine bar has a brick interior giving way to a wood-lined courtyard. Bondi Radio broadcasts live from a booth near the kitchen, which specialises in burgers. It's a cool place with a great weekend vibe. (02-9365 2872; www.neighbourhoodbondi.com.au; 143 Curlewis St, Bondi Beach; 5-11pm Mon-Thu, from 4pm Fri, from noon Sat, 10am-10pm Sun; ; 333, 380-382)

Icebergs Bar

BAR

The neighbouring eatery is more famous, but the casual-chic Icebergs Bar (see 18 ⊗ Map p148, D3) is a brilliant place for a drink. Colourful sofas and ritzy cocktails do little to distract from the killer views from floor-to-ceiling windows looking north across Bondi Beach. A small astroturf terrace adds an outdoor vibe. (☎02-9365 9000; www. idrb.com; 1 Notts Ave, Bondi Beach; ⊙noon-midnight Mon-Sat, 10am-10pm Sun; ☐333, 380-382)

North Bondi RSL

BAR

23 ⊙ MAP P148, F2

This Returned & Services League bar ain't fancy, but with views no one can afford and drinks that everyone can, who cares? The kitchen serves good cheap nosh, including a dedicated kids' menu. Bring ID, as nonmembers theoretically need to prove that they live at least 5km away. Grab a balcony seat for the perfect beach vistas. (☎02-9130 3152; www.northbondirsl. com.au; 120 Ramsgate Ave, North Bondi; ⊙noon-10pm Mon-Thu, noon-11pm Fri, 10am-11pm Sat, 10am-10pm Sun; 🚼; ☐380-382, 379)

Clovelly Hotel

PUB

24 ⊙ MAP P148, C6

A renovated megalith on the hill above Clovelly Beach, this pub has a shady terrace and water views – perfect for post-beach Sunday-afternoon bevvies (drinks). If you fancy being in-doors, the cosy front bar or ultra-spacious lounge will do the trick. Food, now that it's under the Matt Moran empire, is on the up. (☎02-9665 1214; www.clovellyhotel. com.au; 381 Clovelly Rd, Clovelly; ⊙10am-midnight Mon-Sat, to 10pm Sun; ☏; ☐338-9)

Coogee Bay Hotel

PUB

25 ⊙ MAP P148, B8

This enormous, rambling, rowdy complex packs in the backpackers for live music, open-mic nights, comedy and big-screen sports in the beaut beer garden, sports bar and Selina's nightclub. Sit on a stool at the window overlooking the beach and sip on a cold one. (☎02-9665 0000; www.coogeebay hotel.com.au; 253 Coogee Bay Rd, Coogee; ⊙8am-4am Mon-Thu, to 6am Fri & Sat, to 10pm Sun; ☏; ☐313-14, 353, 372-4)

Bucket List

BAR

26 ⊙ MAP P148, E2

By no means subtle, Bucket List blares out beachy pop over its excellent in-demand terrace and promotes a hedonistic good-times atmosphere. Sip on an ice-cold beverage while watching the passing parade or gazing aimlessly out to sea. The interior doesn't lack for views either, with a big wraparound window giving it a conservatory feel. (☎02-9365 4122; www.thebucket listbondi.com; Bondi Pavilion, Bondi Beach; ⊙11am-midnight; ☏; ☐333, 380-2)

Entertainment

Bondi Openair Cinema

CINEMA

27 ⭐ MAP P148, E2

Enjoy open-air screenings by the sea, with live bands providing prescreening entertainment. Online bookings are cheaper and recommended anyway. (www.openaircinemas.com.au; Dolphin Lawn, next to Bondi Pavilion, Bondi Beach; adult/concession $25/17; ⏱mid-Jan–Feb; 🚌333, 380-2)

Shopping

Surfection

FASHION & ACCESSORIES

28 🔒 MAP P148, D2

Selling boardies, bikinis, sunnies, shoes, watches, tees...even luggage – Bondi's coolest surf shop has just about everything the stylish surfer's heart might desire. Old boards hang from the ceiling, while new boards fill the racks. (📞02-9300 6619; 31 Hall St, Bondi Beach; ⏱9.30am-6pm Mon-Wed & Sat, to 9pm Thu, to 7pm Fri, 10am-6pm Sun; 🚌333, 380-382)

Gertrude & Alice

BOOKS

29 🔒 MAP P148, D2

This second-hand bookshop and cafe sees locals, students and academics hang out reading and drinking excellent coffee. Join them for comfort food and discourse around communal tables. (📞02-9130 5155; www.gertrudeandalice.com.au; 46 Hall St, Bondi Beach; ⏱6.45am-9pm; 🛜; 🚌379)

Bondi Markets

MARKET

30 🔒 MAP P148, E1

On Sundays, when the kids are at the beach, their school fills up with characters rummaging through tie-dyed secondhand clothes, original fashion, books, beads, earrings, aromatherapy oils, candles, old records and more. There's a farmers market here on Saturdays (9am to 1pm). (www.bondimarkets.com.au; Bondi Beach Public School, Campbell Pde, Bondi Beach; ⏱10am-4pm Sun, to 5pm Dec & Jan; 🚌380-382)

Aquabumps

ART

31 🔒 MAP P148, D1

Photographer/surfer Eugene Tan has been snapping photos of Sydney's sunrises, surf and sand for 20 years. His colourful prints hang in this cool space, just a splash from Bondi Beach. (📞02-9130 7788; www.aquabumps.com; 151 Curlewis St, Bondi Beach; ⏱10am-6pm; 🚌333, 380-2)

Walking Tour 🥾

A Day in Watsons Bay

The narrow peninsula ending in South Head is one of Sydney's most sublime spots. The view of the harbour from the Bondi approach, as Old South Head Rd leaves the sheer ocean cliffs to descend to Watsons Bay, is breathtaking. Watsons Bay was once a small fishing village, as evidenced by the tiny heritage cottages that pepper the narrow streets.

Getting There

⚓ Regular ferries run between Circular Quay and Watsons Bay.

🚌 Routes to Watsons Bay include the 325 via Vaucluse and the 380 via Bondi.

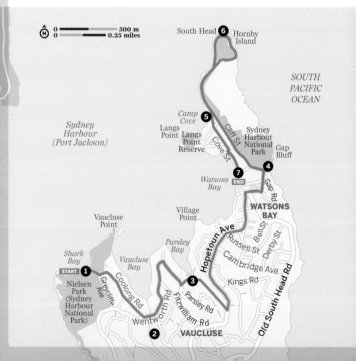

❶ Nielsen Park

Something of a hidden gem, this leafy harbourside **park** (Vaucluse Rd, Vaucluse; ⏱national park area 5am-10pm; 🚌325) with a sandy beach was once part of the 206-hectare Vaucluse House estate. Visit on a weekday when it's not too busy. The park encloses **Shark Beach** – a great spot for a swim, despite the ominous name – and **Greycliffe House**, an 1851 Gothic sandstone pile (not open to visitors).

❷ Vaucluse House

Vaucluse House (📞02-9388 7922; www.sydneylivingmuseums.com.au; Wentworth Rd, Vaucluse; adult/child $12/8; ⏱10am-4pm Wed-Sun; 🚌325) is an imposing specimen of Gothic Australiana set among 10 hectares of lush gardens. Building commenced in 1805 but the house was tinkered with into the 1860s. Decorated with European period pieces, it offers visitors a rare glimpse into early (albeit privileged) colonial life.

❸ Parsley Bay

A hidden gem, this little **bay** (Vaucluse; 🚌325) has a calm swimming beach, a lawn dotted with sculptures for picnics and play, and a cute suspension bridge. Keep an eye out for water dragons as you walk down through the bush.

❹ The Gap

On the ocean side of Watsons Bay, the Gap is a dramatic cliff-top lookout. See if you can spot one of the frequent proposals taking place.

❺ Camp Cove

Immediately north of Watsons Bay, this **swimming beach** (Cliff St, Watsons Bay; 🚌324, 325, 380, ⛴Watsons Bay) is popular with both families and topless sunbathers. When Governor Phillip realised Botany Bay didn't cut it as a site for a settlement, he sailed north into Sydney Harbour, dropped anchor and stepped onto Camp Cove's golden sand on 21 January 1788.

❻ South Head

The **South Head Heritage Trail** passes old battlements and a path heading down to **Lady Bay**, a diminutive gay nudist beach, before continuing on to the candy-striped Hornby Lighthouse and the sandstone Lightkeepers' Cottages (1858) on South Head itself. The harbour views, whale-watching opportunities and crashing surf on the ocean side make this a very dramatic and beautiful spot indeed.

❼ Watsons Bay Beach Club

One of the great pleasures in Sydney life is languishing in the beer garden of the **Watsons Bay Hotel** (📞02-9337 5444; www.watsonsbay hotel.com.au; 1 Military Rd; ⏱10am-midnight Mon-Sat, to 10pm Sun; 🚌324, 325, 380, ⛴Watsons Bay) after a day at the beach. Stay to watch the sun go down over the city. Adjacent **Doyles** (📞02-9337 2007; www.doyles. com.au; 11 Marine Pde, Watsons Bay; mains $41-49; ⏱noon-3pm & 5.30-9pm Mon-Fri, noon-4pm & 5.30-9pm Sat & Sun) is a famous fish restaurant with a takeaway outlet.

Explore ◈

Manly

With both a harbour side and a glorious ocean beach, Manly is Sydney's only ferry destination with surf. Capping off the harbour with scrappy charm, it's a place worth visiting for the ferry ride alone. The surf's good, there are appealing contemporary bars and eateries and, as the gateway to the Northern Beaches, it makes a popular base for the board-riding brigade. There's also some great walking to be done.

The Corso connects Manly's ocean and harbour beaches; here surf shops, burger joints, juice bars and pubs are plentiful. The refurbished Manly Wharf has classier pubs and restaurants, and there are some good cafes and small bars scattered around the back streets.

The great walks on North Head (p162) and the Manly Scenic Walkway (p164) to the Spit Bridge are very worthwhile at any time.

Getting There & Around

🚢 Frequent direct ferries head from Circular Quay to Manly, making this the best (and most scenic) way to go. Regular Sydney ferries take 30 minutes for the journey, while fast ferries take just 18 minutes.

🚌 Express bus E70 takes 35 to 40 minutes to get to Manly Wharf from near Wynyard Station, while its weekend equivalent, the 170, takes longer.

Manly Map on p166

The Corso, connecting Manly's two beaches

Top Sight 📷
North Head

About 3km south of Manly, spectacular North Head offers dramatic cliffs, lookouts, pretty paths through the native scrub and sweeping views of the ocean, the harbour and the city. It's great to explore by bike or on foot. Grab a map and plot your own path through the headland, taking in former military barracks, WWII gun emplacements, a quarantine cemetery and a military memorial walk. At the tip, Fairfax Lookouts offer dramatic clifftop views.

◎ **MAP P166, D5**

✆ 1300 072 757

www.nationalparks.nsw.gov.au

North Head Scenic Dr

admission free

🕐 sunrise-sunset

🚍 135

Viewpoints

Just before the roundabout by the Q Station (p167), take the metal walkway leading off to the left. Follow it up through attractive native scrub, then take a right at the T-junction near the Barracks complex to reach a couple of spectacular viewpoints, one along the Northern Beaches, one across the harbour. The path then arrives at the evocative Third Quarantine Cemetery, with more marvellous harbour vistas.

A Military History

North Head was long a major army base and a key part of Sydney Harbour's defensive system; there are numerous gun emplacements and fortifications. The North Fort complex has a network of tunnels that can be visited by tour as well as an information centre and cafe (open until 4pm). From here begins **Australia's Memorial Walk**, a commemorative brick footpath honouring the armed forces. It passes a series of WWII gun emplacements and links up with a scenic, partly cobbled road that was designed in the 1920s as a WWI memorial.

Fairfax Lookouts

At the end of the headland, a circular track with more defensive fortifications plus information on flora and fauna runs out to the very mouth of Sydney Harbour, where, atop impressive sandstone cliffs, you can gaze your heart out at sea, harbour, city skyline and the parallel bulk of South Head, opposite. Watching one of the big cruise ships sail in or out is quite a sight.

Bluefish Track

The best way to leave is via this spectacular short path that winds across sandstone outcrops, offering magnificent sea views. Squeeze through a low door in a sturdy wall and you'll emerge in the carpark just above Shelly Beach (p167).

★ Top Tips

• At Manly ferry wharf, pick up a map from the Hello Manly information centre as you pass.

• You can walk here easily enough from Manly Wharf, but the 135 bus will also bring you here.

✕ Take a Break

There's a cafe at the North Fort complex in the heart of the headland and eating options at the Q Station (p167).

Finish your exploration by descending the Bluefish Track down to Shelly Beach and tasty seafood at the Boathouse (p169).

Walking Tour 🥾

Manly Scenic Walkway

This epic walk traces the coast west from Manly past million-dollar harbour-view properties and then through a rugged 2.5km section of Sydney Harbour National Park that remains much as it was when the First Fleet sailed in. Make sure you carry plenty of water, slop on some sunscreen, slap on a hat and wear sturdy shoes.

Walk Facts

Start Manly Cove
End Spit Bridge
Length 9km; four hours

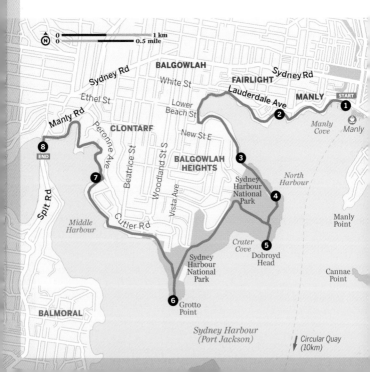

❶ Manly Cove

Pick up a walk brochure (which includes a detailed map) from the visitor information centre by Manly Wharf. Walk along Manly Cove (p168) and find the path at the end of the beach.

❷ Fairlight Beach

After 700m you'll reach Fairlight Beach, where you can scan the view through the heads. Yachts tug at their moorings as you trace the North Harbour inlet for the next 2km.

❸ Forty Baskets Beach

Forty Baskets Beach sits at the point where the well-heeled streets of Balgowlah Heights end and bushclad Sydney Harbour National Park commences. The picnic area is cut off at high tide.

❹ Reef Beach

Kookaburras cackle as you enter the national park and approach Reef Beach, a beautiful cove with turquoise water and great views back to Manly.

❺ Dobroyd Head

The track becomes steep, sandy and rocky further into the park –

keep an eye out for wildflowers, spiders in bottlebrush trees and fat goannas sunning themselves. The views from Dobroyd Head are unforgettable. Check out the deserted 1930s sea shacks at the base of Crater Cove cliff.

❻ Grotto Point

Look for Aboriginal rock carvings on a ledge left of the track before the turn-off to Grotto Point Lighthouse. Rugged and beautiful, Washaway Beach is a secluded little spot on the point's eastern edge.

❼ Clontarf Beach

Becalmed Castle Rock Beach is at the western end of the national park. From here the path winds around the rear of houses to Clontarf Beach, where there's a wide stretch of sand and the walk's only real eating stop.

❽ Spit Bridge

Sandy Bay follows and then Fisher Bay before you reach Spit Bridge, a bascule bridge that connects Manly to Mosman and opens periodically to let boats through to Middle Harbour. From here you can bus back to Manly or into the city.

Manly

Pittwater Rd   23
Raglan St
Ivanhoe Park
Manly
Sydney Rd

1

Manly
Art Gallery
& Museum   7
Manly
Bike
Tours

Belgrave St
9
11
8
17
13
18 10

The Corso
19   1 Manly
Beach

North Steyne

↑ Manly Surf School
(350m)

SOUTH
PACIFIC
OCEAN

Manly
Cove 15
Manly   14
20

1
16
21

Wentworth
St
South
Steyne
Victoria
Pde

22

Cabbage Tree
Bay

Shelly
Beach 4

Shelly
Beach
Park

12

2

Manly
Cove

Manly
Kayak
Centre

East Esp

Ashburner St
Reddall St
Cliff St
Addison Rd

Bower St

MANLY

Darley Rd
High St

Store
Beach
2

6 St Patrick's
College

Sydney
Harbour
National
Park

↖ Circular Quay
(10km)

Cove Ave
Addison Rd
Stuart St
Woods St
Osborne Rd
Marshall St

North Head Scenic Dr

3

Smedleys
Point

Collins
Flat
Beach

Collins Beach Rd

4

Manly
Point

Little
Manly
Point

North
Harbour

North Head Scenic Dr

5

Cannae
Point

3
Q Station

North
Head

For reviews see
◉ Top Sights   p162
◎ Sights   p167
✕ Eating   p168
☕ Drinking   p170
🔒 Shopping   p171

Sydney
Harbour
National
Park

6

Ⓝ 0 ___ 500 m
0 ___ 0.25 miles

Sights

Manly Beach
BEACH

1 MAP P166, B1

Sydney's second most famous beach is a magnificent strand that stretches for nearly two golden kilometres, lined by Norfolk Island pines and midrise apartment blocks. The southern end of the beach, nearest the Corso, is known as South Steyne, with North Steyne in the centre and Queenscliff at the northern end; each has its own surf lifesaving club. (Manly)

Store Beach
BEACH

2 MAP P166, B4

A hidden jewel on North Head, magical Store Beach can only be reached by kayak (you can hire them from Manly Kayak Centre; p170) or boat. It's a breeding ground for **fairy penguins**, so access is prohibited from dusk, when the birds waddle in to settle down for the night. (dawn-dusk; Manly)

Q Station
HISTORIC BUILDING

3 MAP P166, C5

From 1837 to 1984 this sprawling historic complex in beautiful North Head bushland was used to isolate new arrivals suspected of carrying disease. These days it has been reborn as a tourist destination, offering appealing **accommodation** (02-9466 1500; r $259-399; P 135, Manly) and tours. Shuttle buses whisk you from reception down to the wharf,

where there's a lovely beach, a museum in the old luggage store telling the site's story, an information desk and a cafe. Nearby is a bar and restaurant.

The quarantine station was an attempt to limit the spread of cholera, smallpox, influenza and bubonic plague. Passengers were accommodated according to the class of their ticket. Sandstone inscriptions record the names of ships laid up here; gravestones the names of those who never left.Tours run to a daily or weekly schedule and must be prebooked; contact the office. The 2½-hour Ghostly Encounters tour ($49 to $55) runs nightly and rattles some skeletons; three-hour Extreme Ghost Tours ($75) take it a step further and try to summon the spirits. The two-hour daytime Quarantine Station Story tour ($35) highlights the personal stories of those who worked and waited here, while the 45-minute Wharf Wander ($18) is a truncated version for those short on time. (Quarantine Station; 02-9466 1551; www.qstation.com.au; 1 North Head Scenic Dr, Manly; admission free; museum 10am-4pm; 135)

Shelly Beach
BEACH

4 MAP P166, D2

This pretty, sheltered, north-facing ocean cove is an appealing 1km walk from the busy Manly beach strip. The tranquil waters are a protected haven for marine life, so it offers wonderful **snorkelling**. It's a popular place for picnickers. (Bower St, Manly; Manly)

Manly Cove BEACH

5 ◎ MAP P166, A2

Split in two by Manly Wharf, this sheltered enclave has shark nets and calm water, making it a popular choice for families with toddlers. Despite the busy location, the clear waters have plenty of appeal. (🚢Manly)

St Patrick's College HISTORIC BUILDING

6 ◎ MAP P166, C3

Southeast of Manly's centre, this enormous Gothic Revival college (1889) lords over the rooftops from its hillside position. It used to be a seminary but is now a management college; it doubled as Jay Gatsby's house for Baz Luhrmann's 2013 film version of The Great Gatsby. You can roam the grounds and admire the building from outside.

Australian PM Tony Abbott (in office 2013–15) was a student here in the 1980s, which gave rise to his nickname, the Mad Monk. (www.stpatricksestate.org.au; 151 Darley Rd, Manly; ⏱grounds sunrise-sunset; 🚌135, 🚢Manly)

Manly Art Gallery & Museum MUSEUM

7 ◎ MAP P166, A2

A short stroll from Manly Wharf, this passionately managed community gallery maintains a local focus, with changing, locally relevant exhibitions and a small permanent collection that includes an excellent ceramics gallery. There are lots of old Manly photos to peer at too. (☎02-9976 1421; www.northernbeaches.nsw.gov.au; West Esplanade, Manly; admission free; ⏱10am-5pm Tue-Sun; 🚢Manly)

Eating

Chica Bonita MEXICAN $

8 ✖ MAP P166, B1

This upbeat place rises above its unprepossessing location: straddling the end of a dingy shopping arcade, with carpark views. It offers zingy, inventive Mexican fare from lunchtime burritos to evening tacos, with good margaritas and other cocktails on hand to wash them down. It's easiest to enter from the corner of Whistler St and Market Pl. (☎02-9976 5255; www.chicabonita.com.au; Shop 9, 9 The Corso, Manly; tacos $6, other dishes $10-16; ⏱11.30am-3.30pm & 6-10.30pm Tue-Fri, 11am-3.30pm & 5.30-10.30pm Sat & Sun; 🚢Manly)

Barefoot Coffee Traders CAFE $

9 ✖ MAP P166, B1

Run by surfer lads serving fairtrade organic coffee from a closet-sized open-to-the-breeze shop, Barefoot epitomises Manly cool. Food is limited but the Belgian chocolate waffles go magically well with a macchiato. The coffee is deliciously smooth. There's a larger cafe (p169) on Wentworth St. (☎0415 816 061; www.barefootcoffee.com.au; 18 Whistler St, Manly; snacks $3-7; ⏱6.30am-5pm Mon-Fri, 7am-5pm Sat & Sun; 🖋; 🚢Manly)

Barefoot Coffee Traders   CAFE $

10 🚫 MAP P166, B2

Handy for the ferry, this is a larger outpost of the casually excellent Barefoot Coffee. (www.barefootcoffee.com.au; 1 Wentworth St, Manly; light meals $6-19; ⏱6.30am-5pm Mon-Fri, 7.30am-5pm Sat & Sun; 🛜; 🚢Manly)

Good Hope   MODERN AUSTRALIAN $$

11 🚫 MAP P166, B1

Handsomely designed, with a wall of wine and darkly elegant decor, this is a welcome recent Manly arrival. It offers share plates of innovative and surprising quality in an enjoyable relaxed atmosphere. Sunday brunch is a feast at $35, or $65 beefed up with bottomless Mimosas (champagne and orange juice). (📞02-9977 0194; www.goodhopemanly.com.au; 10 Belgrave St, Manly; share plates $16-38; ⏱4-11pm Tue-Fri, 2-11pm Sat, 10.30am-6pm Sun; 🚢Manly)

Boathouse Shelly Beach   CAFE $$

12 🚫 MAP P166, D2

This sweet little spot on pictur-esque Shelly Beach makes a top venue for breakfast juices, brunches, fish 'n' chips, oysters or daily fish specials, served either in the restaurant section or from the kiosk. There's pleasantly shady outdoor seating. No bookings taken. (📞02-9974 5440; www.theboathousesb.com.au; 1 Marine Pde, Manly; kiosk mains $12-19, restaurant mains $18-29; ⏱7am-4pm; 🛜🍴)

Belgrave Cartel   CAFE $$

13 🚫 MAP P166, B1

This established cafe does perhaps Manly's best espresso in a soothing vintage atmosphere with laneway-style outdoor tables. Breakfasts and Sunday brunches are guaranteed to please, as is the selection of Italian share plates. By night, there's an appealing small-bar scene with cocktails and wine. (📞02-9976 6548; www.belgravecartel.com.au; 6 Belgrave St, Manly; small plates $6-18, mains $16-26; ⏱6am-2pm Mon & Tue, 6am-midnight Wed-Fri, 7am-midnight Sat, 7am-10pm Sun; 🛜; 🚢Manly)

Papi Chulo   LATIN AMERICAN $$$

14 🚫 MAP P166, A2

Casually stylish, this light-filled location on Manly Wharf has a vague vibe of the decadent Latin American tropics suggested by its artfully distressed wood and brick, age-spotted mirrors and lazily spinning fans. Drop in for excellent cocktails or order from the short, top-quality menu, with inventive dishes riffing around smoked and barbecued meats and fish, crunchy vegetables and opulent burgers. (📞02-9114 7341; www.merivale.com.au/papichulo; Manly Wharf, Manly; mains $32-45; ⏱noon-10.30pm Mon-Sat, to 9pm Sun; 🍴; 🚢Manly)

Hugos   MODERN AUSTRALIAN $$$

15 🚫 MAP P166, A2

Occupying Manly's primo wharf lo-cation, Hugos has super views from its open windows and sought-after outdoor deck. Relax on the banquette seating and sip a cocktail, then tuck in to delicious pizzas or an Italian-inflected menu of seafood and yummy desserts. It serves pizza all day; it's also a decent place to just slide in for a beer. (📞02-8116 8555; www.hugos.com.au; Manly Wharf, Manly; pizzas $25-29, mains $34-39; ⏰noon-midnight Mon-Fri, 11.30am-midnight Sat & Sun; 🛜; 🚢Manly)

Drinking

Manly Wharf Hotel
PUB

16 🚇 MAP P166, B2

Just along the wharf from the ferry, this remodelled pub is all glass and water vistas, with loads of seating so you've a good chance of grabbing a share of the view. It's a perfect spot for sunny afternoon beers. There's good pub food, too (mains $22 to $30), with pizzas,

fried fish and succulent rotisserie chicken all worthwhile. (📞02-9977 1266; www.manlywharfhotel.com.au; East Esplanade, Manly; ⏰11.30am-midnight Mon-Fri, 11am-1am Sat, 11am-midnight Sun; 🛜🚻; 🚢Manly)

Donny's
COCKTAIL BAR

17 🚇 MAP P166, B1

This two-level bar-restaurant is an atmospheric spot for a great night-time cocktail if you can read the menu in the low-lit speakeasy ambience. Sweet-toothers will love the sugar-and-coffee hit that is the Sticky Date Espresso, while the ginned-up 'detox' option is served to look like you're having a healthy pot of tea in case your personal trainer drops by.

It does some smart fusion food, too, and has regular live bands. (📞02-9977 1887; www.donnys.com.au; 7 Market Lane, Manly; ⏰6-11pm Mon,

---

Out & Active

Manly is a great place to get out on a surfboard and several places near the beach hire out equipment. It's also a popular spot to learn, with **Manly Surf School** (Map p166 📞02-9932 7000; www.manlysurf school.com; North Steyne Surf Club; 🚌136, 139, 🚢Manly) a reliable operator. Other watery activities are also available, including from **Manly Kayak Centre** (Map p166, B2; 📞02-9976 5057; www.manlykayakcentre. com.au; Manly Wharf; hire per 1/2/4/8hr from $25/45/55/75; ⏰9am-5pm; 🚢Manly), **Manly Ocean Adventures** (📞1300 062 659; www.manlyocean adventures.com.au) and **Dive Centre Manly** (Map p166, see 11 🛟; 📞02-9977 4355; www.divesydney.com.au; 10 Belgrave St; ⏰8.30am-6pm Mon-Fri, 8am-6pm Sat & Sun; 🚢Manly).

On land, there are excellent walks available, while **Manly Bike Tours** (Map p166, A2; 📞02-8005 7368; www.manlybiketours.com.au; Belgrave St, Manly; hire per hr/day from $16/33; ⏰9am-6pm Oct-Mar, to 5pm Apr-Sep; 🚢Manly) hires out bikes and provides maps for self-guided tours.

4pm-midnight Tue-Fri, noon-midnight Sat, noon-10pm Sun; Manly)

4 Pines MICROBREWERY

18 MAP P166, B2

Local brewing concern 4 Pines has set up this handsome two-storey venue opposite the ferry wharf. Some of the beer is brewed here, and you can sip it on the balcony while munching on a pulled-pork burger or a range of other pricey but tasty bar fare. Evening-only downstairs has the same menu, but with table service and no outlook. (02-9976 2300; www.4pinesbeer.com.au; 29/43-45 East Esplanade, Manly; 11am-midnight; ; Manly)

Hotel Steyne PUB

19 MAP P166, B1

With something for everyone, the Steyne is a Manly classic that's big enough to get lost in: it's like a village of its own with various bars and eating areas around the sociable central courtyard, which goes loud and late most nights. The rum-focused Moonshine bar has a balcony with beach views. (02-9977 4977; www.hotelsteyne.com.au; 75 The Corso, Manly; 9am-2am Mon-Sat, to 3am Thu, to midnight Sun; ; Manly)

Bavarian BEER HALL

20 MAP P166, A2

At the ferry wharf, this open-sided bar offers numerous local and imported brews. The pork knuckles and pretzels are delicious; sausages are the best option. (02-9977

8088; www.thebavarian.com.au; Manly Wharf, Manly; 11am-midnight Mon-Fri, 9am-midnight Sat & Sun; ; Manly)

Shopping

Budgy Smugglers SPORTS & OUTDOORS

21 MAP P166, B2

This cheeky Northern Beaches swimwear brand appropriates a well-known Australian slang term for Speedos (think it through) and runs with it. Colourful men's and women's swimmers come in national colours, thematic designs or create-your-own. (0404 026 836; www.budgysmuggler.com.au; 22 Darley Rd, Manly; 9am-5pm; Manly)

Manly Life Saving Club SPORTS & OUTDOORS

22 MAP P166, C2

Support this local institution by nipping upstairs to check out its worthwhile surf shop. (02-9977 2742; www.manlylsc.com; South Steyne, Manly; shop 10am-4pm Mon & Fri, 10.30am-4.30pm Tue-Thu, 9.30am-2.30pm Sat, 8am-3.30pm Sun; Manly)

Aloha Surf SPORTS & OUTDOORS

23 MAP P166, B1

This quality surf shop offers longboards, shortboards, bodyboards, skateboards and surfing fashion. The owner is a proper surfer and can give local advice. (02-9977 3777; www.alohasurfmanly.com; 42 Pittwater Rd, Manly; 9am-6pm Fri-Wed, to 7pm Thu; Manly)

Walking Tour

Northern Beaches

Wilder and more distant than Sydney's eastern strands, the Northern Beaches are a must-see, especially for surfers. Although you'll most likely approach them as a day trip, they're very much a part of the city, with the suburbs pushing right up to the water's edge. Some neighbourhoods are ritzier than others, but what they all have in common is a devotion to the beach.

Trip Details

The quickest route to the Northern Beaches is to get the B-Line bus from Wynyard station. Once there, use the 199 bus, which hops along the beach suburbs.

❶ Narrabeen

Immortalised by the Beach Boys in 'Surfin' USA', long, spectacular **Narrabeen** is hard-core surf turf – get some experience before hitting the breaks. At the far northern end of the beach, there's good paddling for young children on the lagoon side of the strand. Back from the centre of the beach, the lagoon has an 8.4km trail and kayaks for hire.

❷ Avalon

Caught in a sandy '70s time warp, **Avalon** is the mythical Australian beach you always dreamed of but could never find. Challenging surf and sloping, tangerine-gold sand have a jutting headland for a backdrop. There's a sea pool at the southern end. Good, cheap eating options abound in the streets behind.

❸ Whale Beach

Walk or bus from Avalon to sleepy **Whale Beach** (Whale Beach Rd, Whale Beach; 🚌199, L90), off the beaten track and well worth seeking out. A paradisiacal slice of deep, orange-tinted sand backed by pines and flanked by steep cliffs, it's a good beach for surfers and families. There's a sea pool at its southern end. High above, **Jonah's** (📞02-9974 5599; www.jonahs. com.au; 69 Bynya Rd, Whale Beach; 2/3/4 courses $88/115/130; ⊙7.30-9am, noon-2.30pm & 6.30-11pm; 🛜; 🚌199, L90) is a noted destination restaurant.

❹ Palm Beach

Long, lovely Palm Beach is a crescent of bliss, famous as the setting for cheesy TV soap *Home & Away*. The suburb has two sides: the magnificent ocean beach, and a pleasant strip on Pittwater, where the calmer strands are good for young kids. From here you can get ferries to other picturesque Pittwater destinations, including glorious **Ku-ring-gai Chase National Park**.

❺ Lunch at the Boathouse

Sit on the large timber deck right by the sand at Pittwater or grab a table on the lawn at Palm Beach's most popular **cafe** (📞02-9974 5440; www.theboathousepb.com.au; Governor Phillip Park; mains $18-29; ⊙7am-4pm; 🛜🅿; 🚌199, L90). The food (try the legendary fish and chips) is nearly as impressive as the views – and that's really saying something. No bookings are taken.

❻ Barrenjoey Lighthouse

This historic sandstone lighthouse (1881; 📞02-9451 3479; www. nationalparks.nsw.gov.au; Palm Beach; admission free; 🚌L90, 199) sits at the northern tip of the peninsula in an annexe of Ku-ring-gai Chase National Park. For the steep hike to the top, take either the shorter stairs or a winding track: majestic views across Pittwater and down the peninsula are worth the effort.

The route starts from the reserve car park at the northern end of Palm Beach. There are no toilets at the top.

Survival Guide

An iconic Sydney ferry arriving in Circular Quay (p31)
POMINOZ/SHUTTERSTOCK ©

Before You Go

Book Your Stay

o Sydney offers a vast quantity and variety of accommodation, especially concentrated in the downtown, Rocks and Darling Harbour areas.

o Even so, the supply shrivels up under the summer sun, particularly around weekends and big events, so be sure to book ahead.

o Prices, even in the budget class, are high; central hotels charge stratospheric rates.

Useful Websites

Destination NSW (www.sydney.com) Official visitors guide.

TripView The handiest app for planning public transport journeys.

Time Out (www.timeout.com/sydney) What's on information and reviews.

Not Quite Nigella (www.notquitenigella.com) Entertaining food blog.

FBI Radio (https://fbiradio.com) Under-

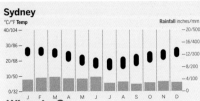

When to Go

o **Summer (Dec–Feb)** The peak season is from Christmas until the end of January, which coincides with summer school holidays and the hot weather.

o **Spring (Sep–Nov)** Usually dry and warm.

o **Autumn (Mar–May)** Sydney's wettest months, but not cold until May.

ground music and arts scene coverage.

Lonely Planet (www.lonelyplanet.com/sydney) Destination information, hotel bookings, traveller forum and more.

Best Budget

Blue Parrot Backpackers (02-9356 4888; www.blueparrot.com.au; 87 Macleay St, Potts Point; dm $40-46; @ ; Kings Cross) As homelike as a hostel can get.

Sydney Harbour YHA (02-8272 0900; www.yha.com.au; 110 Cumberland St; dm $56-64, d $180-250; @ ; Circular Quay) Upmarket hostelling with super harbour views.

Cockatoo Island

(02-8969 2111; www.cockatooisland.gov.au; Cockatoo Island; camp sites $45-50, simple tents $88-99, 2-bed tents $150-175, apt from $265, houses from $625; ; Cockatoo Island) Glamping in the middle of the harbour.

Best Midrange

Tara Guest House (02-9519 4809; www.taraguesthouse.com.au; 13 Edgeware Rd, Enmore; d with/without bathroom $248/215; ; 426) Strikingly good Inner West B&B.

Dive Hotel (02-9665 5538; www.divehotel.com.au; 234 Arden St, Coogee; standard r $215-230, ocean-view r $325-385;

P ♿ ❄ @ 🛜 👶 ;
💻 313-14, 353, 372-3)
Right across from
Coogee Beach.

**Watsons Bay
Boutique Hotel**
(🕽 02-9337 5444; www.
watsonsbay
hotel.com.au; 10 Marine
Pde, Watsons Bay; r
$259-599; P ♿ ❄ 🛜 ;
💻 324-5, 380, ⛴ Wat-
sons Bay) Spacious,
light rooms in a mar-
vellous location.

Best Top End

QT Sydney (🕽 02-8262
0000; www.qthotelsand
resorts.com/sydney-cbd;
49 Market St; r $360-
540; P ♿ ❄ @ 🛜 ;
💻 Queen Victoria Building,
🚆 Town Hall) Stylish,
glamorous, fun and
central.

**ADGE Boutique
Apartment Hotel**
(🕽 02-8093 9888; www.
adgehotel.com.au; 222
Riley St, Surry Hills; apt
$400-650; P ♿ ❄ 🛜 ;
💻 301-2, 352) Check
out that fabulous
carpet!

Ovolo 1888 (🕽 02-
8586 1888; www.ovolo
hotels.com; 139 Murray
St, Pyrmont; r $230-400;
♿ ❄ @ 🛜 ; 💻 Conven-
tion Centre) Brilliant
industrial conversion
near Darling Harbour.

Arriving in Sydney

Sydney Airport

Also known as Kings-
ford Smith Airport,
Sydney Airport (🕽 02-
9667 6111; www.sydneyair
port.com.au; Airport Dr, Mas-
cot), just 10km south
of the centre, has
separate international
(T1) and domestic (T2
and T3) sections, 4km
apart on either side
of the runways. A free
shuttle bus runs be-
tween the two termi-
nals, taking around ten
minutes. They are also
connected by train.
Each has **left-luggage
services** (🕽 02-9667
0926; www.baggagestorage.
com.au; Sydney Airport; 24hr
suitcase/carry-on $16/13),
ATMs, currency-
exchange bureaux and
rental-car counters;
trains, buses and shut-
tles depart from both.

Central Station

Intercity trains pull
into the old ('Country
Trains') section of
Sydney's historic
Central station (Eddy
Ave), in the Haymarket

area of the southern
inner city. From here
you can connect to
the suburban train
network or follow the
signs to Railway Sq
for suburban buses.

Sydney Coach Terminal

Long-distance coach-
es arrive at **Sydney
Coach Terminal** (🕽 02-
9281 9366; 🕐 7am-6pm)
at Central station.
From here you can
access the suburban
train network, buses
and light rail. The
coach terminal office
is upstairs in the main
railway concourse.

Overseas Passenger Terminal

Many cruise ships
dock at the **Overseas
Passenger Terminal**
(🕽 02-9296 4999; www.port
authoritynsw.com) at Cir-
cular Quay, right in the
heart of town, between
the Harbour Bridge
and the Opera House
and near Circular Quay
station. Others pull in
at **White Bay Cruise
Terminal**, in Balmain,
from where ferries and
taxis can run you into
the centre.

Getting Around

Train

o **Sydney Trains** (☏ 13 15 00; www.sydneytrains.info) has a large suburban railway web with relatively frequent services, although there are no lines to the northern or eastern beaches.

o Trains run from around 5am to mid-night – check timetables for your line. They run till a little later at weekends. Trains are replaced by NightRide buses in the small hours. These mostly leave from around Town Hall station and pass through Railway Sq at Central station.

o Trains are significantly more expensive at peak hours, which are from 7am to 9am and 4pm to 6.30pm, Monday to Friday.

o A short one-way trip costs $3.46 with an Opal card, or $2.42 off-peak.

Bus

o **Transport NSW** (☏ 131 500; www.transportnsw. info) has an extensive bus network, operating from around 5am to midnight, when less frequent NightRide services commence.

o Bus routes starting with an M or E indicate express routes; those with an L have similarly limited stops; all are somewhat quicker

The Opal Card

Sydney's public transport network runs on a smartcard system called Opal (www.opal.com.au).

The card can be obtained (for free) and loaded with credit (minimum $10) at numerous newsagencies and convenience stores across Sydney. When commencing a journey you'll need to touch the card to an electronic reader, which are located at the train station gates, near the doors of buses and light-rail carriages, and at the ferry wharves. You then need to touch a reader when you complete your journey so that the system can deduct the correct fare. You get a discount when transferring between services, and after a certain number of journeys in the week, and daily charges are capped at $15.40 ($2.60 on Sundays). You can use the Opal card at the airport train stations, but none of the aforementioned bonuses apply.

You can still buy single tickets (Opal single trip tickets) from machines at train stations, ferry wharves and light-rail stops, or from the bus driver. These are more expensive than the same fare using the Opal card, so there's not much point unless you don't think you'll use $10 worth of transport during your Sydney stay.

You can purchase a child/youth Opal card for those aged four to 15 years; they travel for half price. For student and pensioner discount Opal cards, you have to apply online.

than the regular bus lines.

○ There are several bus hubs in the city centre: Wynyard Park by Wynyard train station; Railway Sq by Central train station; the QVB close to Town Hall station; and Circular Quay by the ferry and train stop of the same name.

○ Use your Opal card to ride buses; tap on when you board, and remember to tap off when you alight, or you'll be charged the maximum fare.

Ferry

○ Most **Sydney ferries** (📞131 500; www.transportnsw.info) operate between 6am and midnight. The standard Opal card one-way fare for most harbour destinations is $5.88; ferries to Manly, Sydney Olympic Park and Parramatta cost $7.35.

○ Private company **Manly Fast Ferry** (📞02-9583 1199; www.manlyfastferry.com.au; adult one-way $9.10) offers boats that blast from Circular Quay to Manly in 18 minutes. Other routes include Manly to Darling Harbour, and an appealing Manly–Watsons Bay–Rose

Bay–Manly route ($15 return). Opal cards are not valid on this service.

○ **Captain Cook Cruises** (📞02-9206 1111; www.captaincook.com.au; Wharf 6, Circular Quay; from $35; 🚢Circular Quay) and **Sydney Harbour Eco-Hopper** (📞02-9583 1199; www.sydneyharboureco hopper.com.au; 24hr pass adult/child $45/25) offer hop-on, hop-off services with several stops around the harbour.

Light Rail (Tram)

○ Trams run between Central station and Dulwich Hill, stopping at Chinatown, Darling Harbour, the Star casino, Sydney Fish Market, Glebe and Leichhardt en route.

○ Opal-card fares cost $2.15 for a short journey and $3.58 for a longer one.

○ A second light rail line will open in 2019. It will run from Circular Quay down a now car-free George St right through the city centre to Central station, then veer east through Surry Hills, past the Sydney Cricket Ground and Sydney Football Stadium and on to Kingsford, with a branch veering to Randwick.

Bicycle

○ Sydney traffic can be intimidating, but there is an increasing number of separated bike lanes; see www.cityofsydney.nsw.gov.au. Helmets are compulsory.

○ Bicycles can travel on suburban trains for free. Bikes also ride for free on Sydney's ferries but are banned from buses.

○ Many cycle-hire shops require a hefty credit-card deposit. For hire, see the following; there are many more operators around town:

Bonza Bike Tours (📞02-9247 8800; www.bonzabiketours.com; 30 Harrington St, the Rocks; tours from $99; ⏰office 9am-5pm; 🚢Circular Quay)

Bike Buffs (📞0414 960 332; www.bikebuffs.com.au; adult/child $95/70; 🚢Circular Quay)

Skater HQ (📞02-8667 7892; www.skaterhq.com.au; 49 North Steyne, Manly; skate & board hire per hr/day $20/30; ⏰9am-6pm Mon-Sat, to 5pm Sun; 🚢Manly)

Manly Bike Tours (📞02-8005 7368; www.

manlybiketours.com.au; Belgrave St, Manly; hire per hr/day from $16/33; ⏱ 9am-6pm Oct-Mar, to 5pm Apr-Sep; 🚢 Manly)

○ Dockless bike-share schemes have taken off in a big way, though their long-term viability has been questioned. Operators are **oBike**, **ofo** and **Reddy Go**; download their apps and ride away.

Car & Motorcycle

Avoid driving in central Sydney if you can: there's a confusing one-way street system, parking's elusive and expensive, and parking inspectors, tolls and tow-away zones proliferate. Conversely, a car is handy for accessing Sydney's outer reaches (particularly the beaches) and for day trips.

Metro

Sydney Metro (www. sydneymetro.info) is a massive new infrastructure project. The first phase, running from Chatswood to Sydney's north-west, should be

operational in 2019. The second phase, linking Chatswood to three new downtown underground stations via a new harbour tunnel and on out to the west, will take longer. Opal cards will be used on the service.

Taxi

○ Metered taxis are easy to flag down in the central city and inner suburbs, except at changeover times (3pm and 3am).

○ Fares are regulated, so all companies charge the same. Flagfall is $3.60, with a $2.50 'night owl surcharge' after 10pm on a Friday and Saturday until 6am the following morning. After that the fare is $2.19 per kilometre, with an additional surcharge of 20% between 10pm and 6am.

○ The ride-sharing app Uber operates in Sydney and is very popular. Other apps such as GoCatch offer ride-sharing and normal taxi bookings, which can be very handy on busy evenings. 13CABS is another nationwide taxi-booking app.

○ For more on Sydney's taxis, see www. nswtaxi.org.au.

Major taxi companies:

Legion Cabs (📞 13 14 51; www.legioncabs. com.au)

Premier Cabs (📞 13 10 17; www.premiercabs. com.au)

RSL Cabs (📞 02-9581 1111; www.rslcabs.com.au)

Silver Service (📞 133 100; www.silverservice. com.au)

Taxis Combined (📞 132 227; www.taxis combined.com.au)

Water Taxi

Water taxis are a fast way to shunt around the harbour (Circular Quay to Watsons Bay in as little as 15 minutes).

Companies will quote on any pick-up point within the harbour and the river, including private jetties, islands and other boats. All have a quote generator on their websites; you can add in extra cruise time for a bit of sightseeing. It's much better value for groups than singles or couples.

Water-taxi companies:

Fantasea Yellow Water Taxis (☏ 1800 326 822; www.yellowwatertaxis.com.au; ⏰ 8am-9pm, prebooking required for service outside these hours)

H2O Maxi Taxis (☏ 1300 420 829; www.h2owatertaxis.com.au)

Water Taxis Combined (☏ 02-9555 8888; www.watertaxis.com.au)

Essential Information

Business Hours

Opening hours vary very widely. The following are approximations:

Restaurants noon to 2.30pm and 6pm to 10pm, sometimes shut Sunday or Monday

Cafes 7am to 4pm

Pubs 11am to midnight Monday to Saturday, noon to 10pm Sunday

Shops 9.30am to 6pm Monday to Wednesday, Friday and Saturday; 9.30am to 8pm

Thursday; 11am to 5pm Sunday

Banks 9.30am to 4pm Monday to Thursday, 9.30am to 5pm Friday

Offices 9am to 5.30pm Monday to Friday

Discount Cards

Sydney Museums Pass (www.sydneylivingmuseums.com.au; adult/child $24/16) Allows a single visit to each of 12 museums in and around Sydney, including the Museum of Sydney, Hyde Park Barracks, Justice & Police Museum and Susannah Place. It's valid for a month and available at each of the participating museums. It costs the same as two regular museum visits.

Ultimate Sydney Pass (adult/child $99/70) Provides access to the high-profile, costly attractions operated by British-based Merlin Entertainment: Sydney Tower Eye (including the Skywalk), Sydney Sea Life Aquarium, Wild

Life Sydney Zoo and Madame Tussauds. It's available from each of the venues, but is often considerably cheaper online through the venue websites. If you plan on visiting only some of these attractions, discounted Sydney Attractions Passes are available in any combination you desire.

Electricity

Type I
230V/50Hz

Standard voltage throughout Australia is 220 to 240 volts AC (50Hz). Plugs are flat three-pin types. You can buy converters for US, European and Asian configurations in airports, outdoors stores, hardware stores, luggage shops and some pharmacies.

Money

There are ATMs everywhere and major credit cards are widely accepted, though there's often a surcharge.

ATMs

Central Sydney is chock-full of banks with 24-hour ATMs that will accept debit and credit cards linked to international networks. Most banks place a A$1000 limit on the amount you can withdraw daily. You'll also find ATMs in pubs and clubs, although these usually charge slightly higher fees. Shops and retail outlets usually have EFTPOS facilities, which allow you to pay for purchases with your debit or credit card; contactless is usually available. Some places like supermarkets offer 'cash out', which means they charge your card more and hand over the difference in cash.

Changing Money

○ Exchange bureaux are dotted around the city centre, Kings Cross and Bondi.

○ Shop around, as rates vary and most charge some sort of commission. The best rates are usually found online.

○ The counters at the airport are open until the last flight comes in; rates here are significantly poorer than they are in the city.

Credit & Debit Cards

Sydneysiders rarely seem to use cash these days, with locals going for contactless 'tap' payments. Visa and MasterCard are widely accepted at shops, restaurants, pubs and hotels. Diners Club and American Express are less widely accepted. A credit card surcharge or minimum transaction amount is common.

Currency

○ The unit of currency is the Australian dollar, which is divided into 100 cents.

○ Notes are colourful,

plastic and washing-machine-proof, in denominations of $100, $50, $20, $10 and $5.

○ Coins come in $2, $1, 50c, 20c, 10c and 5c. The old 2c and 1c coins have been out of circulation for years, so shops round prices up (or down) to the nearest 5c.

○ Travellers cheques are something of a dinosaur these days, and they won't be accepted everywhere. It's easier not to bother with them.

Taxes & Refunds

There's a 10% goods and services tax (GST) automatically added to almost everything you buy, Australia-wide. If you purchase goods with a total minimum value of $300 from any one store within 60 days of departure from Australia, the Tourist Refund Scheme entitles you to a refund of any GST paid (see www.border.gov.au for more information).

Tipping

○ In Sydney most service providers don't

Money-saving Tips

o For views, zip up to **Blu Bar** (☎02-9250 6000; www.shangri-la.com; Level 36, 176 Cumberland St; ⏰5pm-midnight Mon-Thu, 4pm-1am Fri, from 2.30pm Sat, 3-11pm Sun; 🛜; 🚉Circular Quay), on the 36th floor of the Shangri-La hotel, or the rotating O Bar (p73) on the 47th floor of the Australia Square tower. They're not cheap but a cocktail will cost less than the price of visiting Sydney Tower.

o Rather than booking an expensive cruise, explore the harbour on a Manly ferry (p179) or take the Parramatta River service (p52) upstream.

o Instead of the pricey **BridgeClimb** (☎02-8274 7777; www.bridgeclimb.com; 3 Cumberland St; adult $258-383, child $178-273; 🚉Circular Quay), head up the **Pylon Lookout** (☎02-9240 1100; www.pylonlookout.com.au; Sydney Harbour Bridge; adult/child $15/8.50; ⏰10am-5pm; 🚉Circular Quay) instead.

o Save your expensive public transport for Sundays, when all-day Opal card travel costs just $2.60.

---

expect a tip, so you shouldn't feel pressured into giving one.

o The exception is restaurants, where a tip of 10% or so is standard.

o People tend to round up to the nearest dollar or more in taxis.

o Tipping in bars is uncommon but on the increase, especially if there's fancy cocktail wizardry involved.

Public Holidays

On public holidays, government departments, banks, offices and post offices shut up shop. On Good Friday, Easter Sunday, Anzac Day and Christmas Day, most shops are closed.

New Year's Day
1 January

Australia Day
26 January

Easter (Good Friday, Easter Saturday, Easter Monday) March/April

Anzac Day 25 April

Queen's Birthday
Second Monday in June

Labour Day First Monday in October

Christmas Day
25 December

Boxing Day
26 December

o Many public holidays cleverly morph into long weekends (three days), and if a major holiday such as New Year's Day falls on a weekend, the following Monday is a holiday.

o Something else to consider when planning a Sydney visit is school holidays, when accommodation rates soar and everything gets hectic. Sydney students have a long summer break that includes Christmas and most of January. Other school holidays fall around March to April (Easter), late June to mid-July, and late September to early October.

Dos & Don'ts

Greetings Greet both men and women by shaking hands or a kiss/air kiss for friends (it's not custom for straight Aussie blokes to kiss each other though).

Dinner Bring wine, flowers or chocolates if you are invited to someone's house for a meal.

Restaurants Splitting restaurant bills is standard practice.

Parties If you're asked to 'bring a plate' to a party, it means bring food.

Public Transport Offer seats on crowded buses, trains and ferries to older people or parents with kids.

Bargaining Not usual in shops but sometimes OK at some markets.

Escalators Stand on the left, walk on the right.

Safe Travel

○ Sydney's beaches must be treated with healthy respect. People drown every year from rips and currents. Swim between the flags.

○ Police in Sydney have little tolerance for minor transgressions or drug use. Random searches are common in clubs and random drug testing is now conducted on drivers.

○ Sydney's sun is fierce in summer – do as the locals do, applying a hat and plenty of sunscreen.

Toilets

○ Public toilets are free, but there aren't that many of them around.

○ Stations, parks and shopping centres are good bets.

Tourist Information

City of Sydney Information The council operates a good tourist information desk in the **Customs House** (Alfred St, Circular Quay; ⊙ 9am-8pm Mon-Fri, to 5pm Sat & Sun;

🚇 Circular Quay) as well as kiosks in **Martin Place** (⊙ 9am-5pm daily, to 9pm Fri & Sat mid-Nov–mid-Feb; 🚇 Martin Place), **Chinatown** (Dixon St, Haymarket; ⊙ 11am-7pm daily, until 9pm Fri & Sat Nov-Feb; 🚇 Town Hall) and **Kings Cross** (☎ 0477 344 125; cnr Darlinghurst Rd & Springfield Ave, Kings Cross; ⊙ 9am-5pm daily, to 9pm Fri & Sat mid-Nov–mid-Mar; 🚇 Kings Cross).

Sydney Visitor Centre – The Rocks (☎ 02-8273 0000; www.sydney.com; cnr Argyle & Playfair Sts; ⊙ 9.30am-5.30pm, to 6pm Dec & Jan; 🚇 Circular Quay) Sydney's principal tourist office is in the heart of the historic Rocks district

Hello Manly (☎ 02-9976 1430; www.hellomanly.com.au; East Esplanade, Manly; ⊙ 9am-5pm Mon-Fri, 10am-4pm Sat & Sun; ⛴ Manly) This helpful visitors centre, just outside the ferry wharf and alongside the bus interchange, has free pamphlets covering the **Manly Scenic Walkway** (www.manly.nsw.gov.au; ⛴ Manly) and other Manly attractions, plus loads of local bus information.

Parramatta Heritage & Visitor Information Centre (☎ 02-8839 3311; www.discoverparramatta.com; 346a Church St, Parramatta; ⏱ 9am-5pm; ☒ Parramatta) Knowledgeable staff will point you in the right direction with loads of brochures and leaflets, info on access for visitors with impaired mobility, and details on local Aboriginal cultural sites.

Travellers with Disabilities

Compared with many other major cities, Sydney has great access for citizens and visitors with disabilities. Central districts and suburban centres are well endowed with kerb cuts and tactile pavement indicators.

Download Lonely Planet's free Accessible Travel guide from http://lptravel.to/AccessibleTravel.

Hearing-impaired travellers Most of Sydney's major attractions offer hearing loops and some can arrange sign-language interpreters. To make sure your needs can be met, contact venue staff in advance.

Vision-impaired travellers Many new buildings incorporate architectural features that are helpful, such as tactile floor indicators at the top and bottom of stairs. Sydney's pedestrian crossings feature catchy beep-and-buzz sound cues.

Wheelchair access Most of Sydney's main attractions are accessible by wheel-

chair, and all new or renovated buildings must, by law, include wheelchair access. Older buildings can pose some problems, however, and some restaurants and entertainment venues aren't quite up to scratch. Most of the National Trust's historic houses are at least partially accessible.

Parking permits Contact **Roads & Maritime Services** (☎ 13 22 13; www.rms.nsw.gov.au), who can supply temporary parking permits for international drivers with disabilities.

Visas

All visitors to Australia need a visa – only New Zealand nationals are exempt, and even they receive a 'special category' visa on arrival.

Index

See also separate subindexes for:

⊗ **Eating p188**
⊙ **Drinking p189**
✪ **Entertainment p190**
⊙ **Shopping p190**

Behind the Scenes

Send Us Your Feedback

We love to hear from travellers – your comments help make our books better. We read every word, and we guarantee that your feedback goes straight to the authors. Visit **lonelyplanet.com/contact** to submit your updates and suggestions.

Note: We may edit, reproduce and incorporate your comments in Lonely Planet products such as guidebooks, websites and digital products, so let us know if you don't want your comments reproduced or your name acknowledged. For a copy of our privacy policy visit lonelyplanet.com/privacy.

Andy's Thanks

It's always a great pleasure roaming around Sydney, thanks to many extremely helpful people along the way. I am particularly grateful to Corinna Mazurek for excellent cafe investigations, to Toni Sheridan, Daniel Beech, Portia Tshegofatso Loeto, Matt Beech and Peter Smith for sterling research company, to Raquel Bloom and colleagues for so much information, to my family for their support, and to Tasmin Waby and Niamh O'Brien at LP.

Acknowledgements

Cover photograph: Sydney Opera House, Palle Nielsen/500px © Photographs pp26–7 (from left): Nenad Basic/Shutterstock, M. Letscher/Shutterstock, Kompasskind.de/Shutterstock ©

This Book

This 5th edition of Lonely Planet's *Pocket Sydney* guidebook was researched and written by Andy Symington. The previous two editions were written by Peter Dragicevich. This guidebook was produced by the following:

Destination Editors
Niamh O'Brien, Tasmin Waby

Series Designer
Campbell McKenzie

Cartographic Series Designer Wayne Murphy

Senior Product Editor Kate Chapman

Product Editor Heather Champion

Senior Cartographer Julie Sheridan

Book Designer Gwen Cotter

Assisting Editors Melanie Dankel, Rebecca Dyer, Trent Holden, Ali Lemer, Lorna Parkes, Monique Perrin

Cover Researcher Brendan Dempsey-Spencer

Thanks to Imogen Bannister, Laura Crawford, Blaze Hadzik, James Hardy, Liz Heynes, Simon Hoskins, Chris Lee Ack, Jean-Pierre Masclef, Liam McGrellis, Dan Moore, Virginia Moreno, Darren O'Connell, Martine Power, Kirsten Rawlings, Wibowo Rusli, Dianne Schallmeiner, Ellie Simpson, Victoria Smith, John Taufa, Angela Tinson, Juan Winata

Our Writer

Andy Symington

Andy has written or worked on more than a hundred books and other updates for Lonely Planet (especially in Europe and Latin America) and other publishing companies, and has published articles on numerous subjects for a variety of newspapers, magazines and websites. He part-owns and operates a rock bar, has written a novel and is currently working on several fiction and nonfiction writing projects. Andy first became involved in writing when someone cannily contracted him to contribute to a pub guide: his formidable research on that title broke a man but launched a career.

Originally from Australia, Andy moved to northern Spain many years ago. When he's not off with a backpack in some far-flung corner of the world, he can probably be found watching the tragically poor local football side or tasting local wines after a long walk in the nearby mountains.

Published by Lonely Planet Global Limited
CRN 554153
5th edition – October 2018
ISBN 978 1 78657 270 7
© Lonely Planet 2018   Photographs © as indicated 2018
10 9 8 7 6 5 4 3 2 1
Printed in Malaysia